TINY
DINO
WORLDS

TINY DINO WORLDS

Create Your Own Prehistoric Habitats

CHRISTINE BAYLES KORTSCH, PhD

with JUSTIN TWEET, MS, and KAREN CHIN, PhD

ROOST BOOKS

Roost Books
An imprint of Shambhala Publications, Inc.
4720 Walnut Street
Boulder, Colorado 80301
roostbooks.com

© 2020 by Christine Bayles Kortsch

All photographs are by the author except those by Kristen Hatgi on pages p. ii (second photo), xiv, xvi, xviii (first photo), xx, xxii, xxviii, 4, 10, 14, 20, 25, 32, 37, 42, 47, 52, 56, 62, 67, 72, 77, 96, 100, 131, and 148. Photo of aspen trees on page 71 by Daniel Kortsch.

Graphics on pages xi, xii, xiv by Sumana Ghosh-Witherspoon.

9 8 7 6 5 4 3 2 1

First Edition
Printed in China

♾ This edition is printed on acid-free paper that meets the American National Standards Institute Z39.48 Standard.
♻ Shambhala Publications makes every effort to print on recycled paper. For more information please visit www.shambhala.com.

Roost Books is distributed worldwide by Penguin Random House, Inc., and its subsidiaries.

Cover and book design by Shubhani Sarkar, sarkardesignstudio.com

Library of Congress Cataloging-in-Publication Data

Names: Kortsch, Christine Bayles, author.
Title: Tiny dino worlds: create your own prehistoric habitats / Christine Bayles Kortsch, PhD with Karen Chin, PhD, and Justin Tweet, MS.
Description: First edition. | Boulder: Roost Books, an imprint of Shambhala Publications, Inc., 2020. | Includes bibliographical references and index.
Identifiers: LCCN 2018040170 | ISBN 9781611805864 (paperback: alk. paper)
Subjects: LCSH: Dinosaurs.
Classification: LCC QE861.4 .K67 2020 | DDC 567.9—dc23
LC record available at https://lccn.loc.gov/2018040170

For Daniel, Jack,
and Owen,
with all my love

CONTENTS

WELCOME TO THE MESOZOIC! **xi**

DINO WORLDS 101 **xvii**

CH. 1
HERDS OF A FEATHER FLOCK TOGETHER
Coelophysis 1

Fallen Log Terrarium **5**

Dragonfly in Amber **8**

CH. 2
TRACKS
Behavior but No Bones 11

Sand Ribbons Terrarium **15**

Baked Tracks **19**

CH. 3
UNDER THE SEA
Plesiosaurus 21

Underwater Terrarium **24**

Salt Dough Ammonite **29**

CH. 4
JURASSIC GIANTS
Stegosaurus, Allosaurus, and *Apatosaurus* 33

Box Terrarium **36**

Designer Dinos **40**

CH. 5
DOWN BY THE SEASHORE
Tapejara Takes to the Skies 43

Seaside Terrarium **46**

Colored Sand **50**

CH. 6
DINO DOO-DOO
Everybody Poops, Even *Maiasaura* 53

Forest Floor Terrarium **57**

Coprolites (Dino Poop) **61**

CH. 7

CRETACEOUS CLASH
Tyrannosaurus Rex and Triceratops Fight to the Death   63

Cliffside Battle Terrarium   **66**

Leaf Hunt and Gratitude Tree   **70**

CH. 8

DINO MUMMIES AND WORMY CARCASSES
What Happens When a Brachylophosaurus Dies?   73

River Run Terrarium   **76**

Stuck in the Slime   **80**

CH. 9

END OF THE WORLD
After All the Titanosaurs Died   83

Erupting Volcano Terrarium   **87**

Papier-Mâché Volcano   **93**

CH. 10

DINO DIG
Aardonyx to Zuul   97

Utah Dinosaur Dig   **101**

Fossil Impression with Homemade Modeling Clay   **105**

CH. 11

PARTY TIME
How to Throw a Dino-Tastic Gathering   107

Mini Dino Terrariums   **109**

Dinosaur Ice Eggs   **112**

Sew a Dino Card   **117**

Sandbox Dino Dig   **120**

Dino Stamp Wrapping Paper   **123**

Volcano Ice Cream Cake   **124**

ACKNOWLEDGMENTS   **130**

INTERVIEW: KIDS ASK . . .   **133**

DINOS IN DETAIL   **137**

INDEX   **140**

ABOUT THE AUTHOR AND CONTRIBUTORS   **146**

WELCOME TO THE MESOZOIC!

Everyone loves dinosaurs! These fascinating creatures stomped, strolled, or skittered about during the Mesozoic Era. That's about 252 to 66 million years ago (mya). More than 1,500 species of extinct Mesozoic dinosaurs have been named. Paleontologists are learning more about dinosaurs every day.

Did you know that dinosaurs didn't live alone? Although they grab most of the attention,

dinosaurs lived with many other types of animals and plants. Paleontologists have also learned a lot about the climates and plants of the Mesozoic. This book will help you create your own dinosaur scenes based on the most recent scientific evidence. Have fun building a living dinosaur world in your own home. Then teach your friends about the science behind your ancient scene.

DINOSAUR TIMELINE

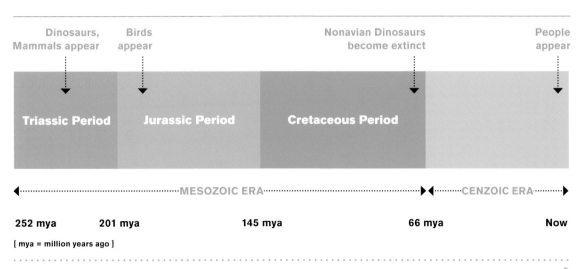

Dinosaurs, Mammals appear	Birds appear		Nonavian Dinosaurs become extinct	People appear
Triassic Period	**Jurassic Period**	**Cretaceous Period**		

◄ ·········· MESOZOIC ERA ··········► ◄ ········· CENZOIC ERA ·········►

252 mya   **201 mya**   **145 mya**   **66 mya**   **Now**

[mya = million years ago]

TIMELINE OF THE MESOZOIC ERA

EPOCH   **EVENTS**

Cretaceous Period 145–66 mya

Late Cretaceous
100–66 mya

▶ End-Cretaceous extinction kills off nonavian dinosaurs, pterosaurs, plesiosaurs, mosasaurs, ichthyosaurs, ammonites, and others

▶ Giant volcanic eruptions in India

▶ Rocky Mountains begin to take shape

▶ First true crocodilians and snakes

Early Cretaceous
145–100 mya

▶ First flowering plants, social insects, and mosasaurs

▶ Birds diversify

▶ The southern continents split into South America, Africa, Antarctica + Australia, and India + Madagascar

▶ Shallow continental seas submerge low areas of continents

Jurassic Period 201–145 mya

Late Jurassic
163–145 mya

▶ True mammals and salamanders

▶ Dinosaurs experimenting with flight

Middle Jurassic
174–163 mya

▶ Most of the initial groups of dinosaurs have gone extinct

Early Jurassic
201–174 mya

▶ True frogs

▶ North and South America separate

▶ Dinosaurs diversify

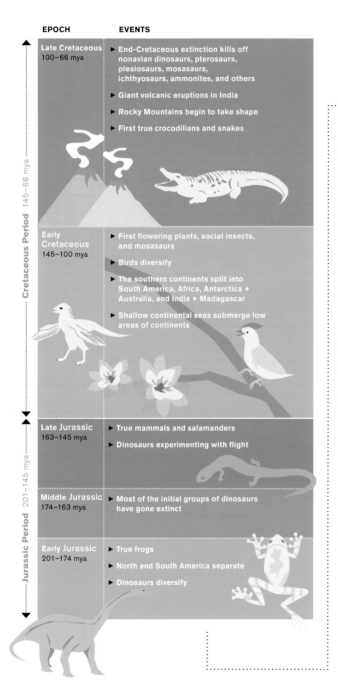

Triassic Period 252–201 mya

Late Triassic
237–201 mya

▶ End-Triassic extinction wipes out many reptile groups

▶ Pangaea begins to separate at future North Atlantic

▶ Many groups appear: first dinosaurs, pterosaurs, plesiosaurs, turtles, and lizards, plus close cousins to mammals and crocodiles

Middle Triassic
247–237 mya

▶ Appearance of modern corals

▶ First true ichthyosaurs

Early Triassic
252–247 mya

▶ Recovery from mass extinctions at end of previous Permian Period

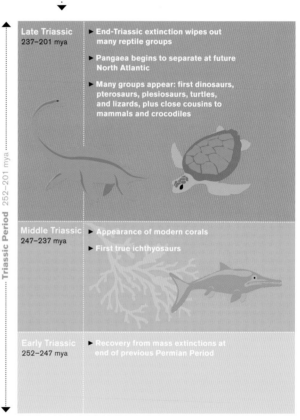

DINOSAURS AND THEIR WORLD

The oldest known dinosaur fossils are between 230 and 225 million years old, from the beginning of the Late Triassic Period. Those early dinosaurs were small and uncommon. They lived in a world dominated by many kinds of unusual reptiles, amphibians, and mammal relatives.

Over the rest of the Triassic, new types of dinosaurs appeared and became more common. A mass extinction at the end of the Triassic cleared the way for dinosaurs to dominate the land while many other animals died out. Dinosaurs spread over all of the continents. Some became the largest animals ever to walk the earth.

But the time of the dinosaurs didn't last forever. The great Mesozoic dinosaurs went extinct 66 million years ago, when a huge impact from outer space and vast volcanic eruptions in India caused the extinctions of at least 60 percent of organisms on Earth. Fortunately, some dinosaurs survived to live with us today—birds. That's right! Birds are living dinosaurs.

Sometimes people call any big extinct animal a dinosaur. This isn't true! Birds are dinosaurs, but pterosaurs were *not* dinosaurs. Dinosaurs didn't live in water, so swimming ichthyosaurs and plesiosaurs were *not* dinosaurs. Dinosaurs had special anatomical features, so animals such as *Dimetrodon* that looked like dinosaurs but lived in the older Permian were *not* dinosaurs. Extinct mammals such as mammoths and glyptodonts were *not* dinosaurs.

Another thing that might surprise you is that not all dinosaurs were big. People get excited about vicious *Tyrannosaurus rex* or massive *Argentinosaurus,* but many species were less than 10 feet long and weighed less than an average adult human. Most dinosaurs can be divided into one of following groups (for more details, see "Dinos in Detail," page 137):

- **Theropods:** bipedal (walking on two legs) hunters that include birds; most famous as carnivores, with sharp teeth and large claws, but some were omnivores or even herbivores

- **Sauropodomorphs:** heavy animals with long necks and long tails; mostly herbivores with a few omnivores

- **Ornithischians:** also called beaked dinosaurs because they had a special beak-forming bone on the lower jaw; mostly herbivores with a few omnivores

The world changed a lot over the millions of years of the Mesozoic Era. The continents began the Mesozoic as one supercontinent, called Pangaea, which allowed plants and animals to spread easily. By the end of the Mesozoic, Pangaea had broken up into the modern continents, which looked a lot like they do today except India was a giant island slowly moving north. Many familiar groups of plants and animals—including frogs,

WHAT'S FOR DINNER?

What is the difference between a carnivore, an herbivore, and an omnivore?
- Carnivore: **meat eater**
- Herbivore: **plant eater**
- Omnivore: **plant and meat eater**

turtles, lizards, snakes, and crocodiles—got their start in the Mesozoic as well. True mammals appeared but were probably only active at night. Birds (also known as avian dinosaurs) appeared during the Jurassic and joined the flying pterosaurs in the air. Flowering plants also appeared during the Mesozoic, and new kinds of insects evolved along with them.

PANGAEA

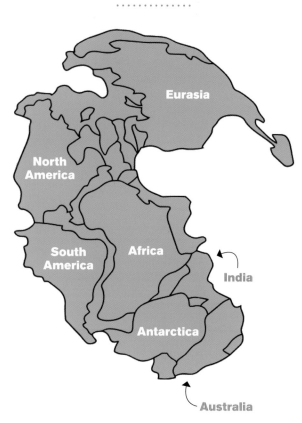

WHERE ARE DINOSAURS FOUND?

Dinosaur fossils are found in sediment that accumulated over long periods of time. In geology, a formation is a layer of rock or sediment. The material of a formation was all deposited in a particular region within a period of geologic time and in the same general setting. For example, the Morrison Formation is a famous formation in western North America. All of the rocks were deposited over a few million years, mostly in rivers, floodplains, and lakes. Different formations are found above and below the Morrison. Formations often have characteristic fossils. Most of the chapters in this book focus on specific formations.

Today, paleontologists study dinosaur fossils from all around the world, in rock formations from deep in Antarctica to the Sahara and everywhere in between. Maybe one day you'll study these rare and wonderful creatures from another time!

COMMON FORMATIONS

NAME	PLACE	AGE	KNOWN FOR	CHAPTER
Lameta Formation	Western and central India	Late Cretaceous, 66 million years ago	Titanosaurs, giant snakes	9
Hell Creek Formation and Lance Formation	Western United States	Late Cretaceous, 68 to 66 million years ago	*Tyrannosaurus* and *Triceratops*	7
Two Medicine Formation	Montana, United States	Late Cretaceous, 77 to 76 million years ago	*Maiasaura*, dinosaur eggs and babies	6
Judith River Formation	Montana, United States	Late Cretaceous, 78 to 76 million years ago	*Brachylophosaurus*	8
Santana Formation	Northeastern Brazil	Early Cretaceous, 100 million years ago	Pterosaurs, spinosaurs	5
Morrison Formation	Western United States	Late Jurassic, 156 to 146 million years ago	*Allosaurus*, *Stegosaurus*, many sauropods	4
Lias Group	Southern England	Early Jurassic, 200 to 180 million years ago	*Ichthyosaurus*, *Plesiosaurus*	3
Navajo Sandstone and the rest of the Glen Canyon Group	Southwestern United States	Early Jurassic, 202 to 174 million years ago	Dinosaur tracks	2
Chinle Formation	Southwestern United States	Late Triassic, 225 to 202 million years ago	*Coelophysis*, petrified wood	1

DINO WORLDS 101

Welcome to *Tiny Dino Worlds!* Have you picked out the project you want to make first? Each chapter of this book focuses on a different dinosaur, formation, time period, or ecosystem. Plant a lush tropical Wardian case for a clashing battle between *Tyrannosaurus rex* and *Triceratops*. (What on earth is a Wardian case, you might ask? Turn to chapter 7 to find out!) Design a sand ribbons terrarium with baked dinosaur "tracks" and rootless air plants. Create a woodland scene with ferns, moss, and a trickling stream. These projects are designed for kids, but anyone who loves dinosaurs will have fun creating miniature prehistoric habitats.

Each project offers a modern interpretation of what different dinosaurs' environments may have looked like. This means we will steer you toward plants that resemble their prehistoric relatives. You'll learn a ton about dinosaurs—some you already know and love, and some you've never heard of. We'll teach you about prehistoric geology and ecosystems, not to mention paleobotany, which is the science of prehistoric plants. Have fun wowing friends and family with all your new knowledge.

These projects are educational, but they are also works of living, interactive art. Terrariums and miniature gardens are all the rage. Display your creation proudly on a sunny coffee table, adding instant whimsy and beauty to your home. Set your habitat on the dining room table and play with it. Dream up imaginary battlegrounds, nests, and hiding places for your dinosaurs. Take what you learn and put your own unique spin on each dino world.

Above all, we hope these projects will inspire shared creativity and a deep love of nature. Did you know that plants literally clean the air in our homes? Nature calms us down and connects us to the mystery of the universe. Bring a splash of the natural world into your home. In a world that's go-go-go, carve out a few hours to sit down with a friend or family member to create a miniature habitat side by side. You'll find infinite pleasure in making simple things with your hands. Slow down and take joy in the act of making something beautiful with those you love.

SAFETY FIRST

These projects are for anyone who loves dinosaurs—from young children to grown-ups. Please note that some of the projects involve tools that are not safe for young children (butter knives, glass containers, the stove, and small objects such as glass beads). The directions for each project include options so that you can pick the container, tools, decorations, and method that are appropriate for you. Young children should always work with adult supervision. Use your common sense and have fun!

Ready to get started? Let's do this. But before you dive in, here are some tips to make the process fun and enjoyable for everyone.

DINOSAURS

No dino world is complete without an awesome dinosaur toy. To make these projects simple and budget friendly, we've chosen dinosaurs that are either easy to find or to find substitutes for. Feel free to splurge on any specialty dinosaurs that catch your eye, but know that if you buy a basic tube or bucket of miniature dinosaurs, you'll have the dinosaur toys you need for the projects in this book.

WORKSPACE

Before you start opening soil bags and spilling sand, take a few minutes to set up a workspace. Choose a kitchen table, a spot on the floor, or an outdoor patio. Cover your surface with reusable plastic tablecloths, an old sheet, brown craft paper, or newspaper—anything that will protect your space and make cleanup a breeze.

CONTAINERS

Each of these projects calls for a different container. Metal trays, glass-house terrariums, large shallow bowls, wooden planters, plastic storage tubs, white casserole dishes? Yes to all of the above! Glass terrariums and dish gardens come in all different shapes and sizes and they look gorgeous, but they may not be the best choice for younger children. A laminated tray or a lined wooden planter can be repurposed as an attractive dino world (and it does double duty as a sensory bin). Little hands can reach in easily to play, and there's no risk of broken glass.

Bear in mind that succulents will rot quickly in a wet, enclosed terrarium. Air plants need good air circulation, along with regular misting. If you don't have the exact same container as the one recommended, that's fine. Just make sure to choose one that provides similar growing conditions for the ecosystem you're creating.

One last thing—this one is important: Choose a container the adults find attractive. If the grown-ups don't like the look of the container, it will soon be relegated to a dusty corner. Spend a little time finding a container everyone loves. That way, each project will become not only a living diorama for sensory play but also a stunning centerpiece to brighten your home.

PLANTS

Each chapter will focus on specific plants with specific needs. Scout out a local nursery with a terrarium or fairy garden section. Ask a gardener for help, and you'll learn a ton. To get you started, here is a list of good look-alike plants for your prehistoric worlds.

MODERN PLANT LOOK-ALIKES

FOSSIL PLANTS OF THE TRIASSIC, JURASSIC, AND CRETACEOUS PERIODS	MODERN PLANT LOOK-ALIKES
Moss	Pincushion moss (*Leucobryum glaucum*) Delicate fern moss (*Thuidium delicatulum*) Haircap moss (*Polytrichum commune*) Spanish moss (*Tillandsia usneoides*)
Fern	Miniature Boston fern (*Nephrolepis exaltata* 'Mini Russells') Spider fern (*Arachnoides simplicior* 'Variegata') Maidenhair fern (*Adiantum pedatum*) Lemon button fern (*Nephrolepis cordifolia*)
Club mosses (*Lycopodium*)	Golden spikemoss (*Selaginella kraussiana* 'Aurea') Spikemoss (*Selaginella bryopteris*)
Horsetail	Horsetail (*Equisetum hyemale*) Lucky "bamboo" (*Dracaena braunii*) African spear plant (*Sansevieria cylindrica*)
Conifer	Variegated artillery fern (*Pilea microphylla* 'Variegata') Miniature lemon cypress (*Cupressus macrocarpa* 'Goldcrest') Tansu Japanese cedar (*Cryptomeria japonica* 'Tansu') Baby blue Sawara cypress (*Chamaecyparis pisifera* 'Baby Blue') Asparagus plumosa fern (*Asparagus setaceus; Asparagus plumosus*) Norfolk Island pine (*Araucaria heterophylla*) Ming Aralia (*Polyscias fruticosa* 'Snowflake') Haworthia-leaved aloe (*Aloe haworthioides*)
Cycads	Parlor palm (*Chamaedorea elegans*)
Ginkgoes	Dwarf variegated ginkgo (*Ginkgo biloba* 'Majestic Butterfly') Purple or green miniature shamrock without flowers (*Oxalis regnellii*)
FOSSIL PLANTS OF THE CRETACEOUS PERIOD ONLY	MODERN PLANT LOOK-ALIKES
Flowering plants and palms	Miniature African violet (*Saintpaulia ionantha*) Sensitive plant (*Mimosa pudica*) Three-leaf palm (*Licuala triphylla*) Baby tears (*Soleirolia soleirolii*) Elfin thyme (*Thymus minimus* 'Elfin') Creeping fig (*Ficus pumila*) Miniature Japanese holly (*Ilex crenata* 'Jersey Jewel') Dwarf English boxwood (*Buxus sempervirens* 'Suffruticosa') Dwarf elm (*Ulmus parvifolia* 'Hokkaido' or 'Seiju') Miniature sedums (there are tons to choose from!)

Layer Cake Method

All of our dino worlds are planted in containers with no drainage hole. Unless you're working with air plants or aquatic aplants, that means you need to mimic the action of drainage. How? The layer cake method!

1. Always start by washing your container with soap and hot water. Allow to dry. A dirty container can introduce pests and disease, so don't skip this step. If your container can't be washed, wipe it out and let it sit in direct sunshine for a few hours.

2. Begin with a drainage layer. Pea gravel, crushed river rock, aquarium gravel, or small pebbles all work well. If your gravel has been sitting on a shelf for a long time, it will be really dusty. Give it a good rinse in a colander or sieve before adding it to your container.

3. Add a sprinkle of activated horticultural charcoal (found in garden centers). This addition is especially important in closed or semiclosed tropical terrariums to filter out toxic chemicals and keep the terrarium smelling fresh. Charcoal can stain your clothes and hands, so use a scoop, gloves, or a funnel (or make one by folding a paper plate in half).

4. If you're using a clear container, add a band of perlite. Perlite will keep the soil (next layer!) from sliding into the drainage layer and turning it muddy. (If your container isn't see-through, you can skip this step because no one will see your layers anyway.) You could substitute sphagnum moss, a coffee filter, or a piece of weed cloth, but perlite is easy, attractive, cheap, and available in most garden centers.

5. If you like, this is a good time to create extra layers that look pretty from the side. (Again, this is only worth it when using a clear container.) In addition to the basic formula of pea gravel, charcoal, and perlite, you can experiment with contrasting colors of gravel; tiny glittery stones; or white, black, or colored sand. In a very tall container, you could go wild and do thin layers of

pea gravel, charcoal, perlite, soil, sand or glittery gravel, more perlite, then more soil. Have fun! As long as you include some kind of drainage, there really isn't a right or wrong way to do this. That said, perlite is probably the easiest choice to finish your drainage layers and keep the soil from ruining your decorative bands.

6. Scoop in a layer of dampened potting mix. Make sure to choose a soil that's appropriate for your plants. Succulents need a special succulent or cactus mix. Ferns and mosses will thrive in moisture-rich potting soil.

7. Now comes the fun part! Create any landscape features such as hills, cliffs, ponds, rivers, islands, or caves. Use rocks, moss, shells, sticks, feathers, gemstones, seedpods, beads, marbles, or any other found objects you like. Set your potted plants on top of the soil and move them around until you're pleased with the layout.

8. Once you're happy with your overall design, it's time to plant. Make sure your chosen plants all share similar light and moisture needs. Pinch your plants out of the plastic pots they came in. Look at the roots. Are they root-bound (tangled into tight knots)? If so, gently open the roots and spread them out. Dig holes (try not to disrupt your drainage layers), position your plants, and add soil (up to the level of the soil in the original pot). Use your fingers to tamp down the soil around the base of the plants. You'll be surprised how many air pockets will be hiding under what looks like plenty of soil. Keep adding soil and pressing down gently until there are no gaps or holes and the plants are sturdy.

9. Feel free to add more pea gravel, small stones, or live moss to the top layer for a more polished look. Preserved dyed moss is beautiful and fun to work with, but it can introduce mold and suffocate your plants, so use sparingly, especially around the base of your plants.

10. Brush or rinse off any dirt on the leaves. If the plants are wobbly or sticking halfway up out of the dirt, the roots won't get established. If the leaves are smothered in soil or smashed against the container edge, they will rot. Take a few moments now to give your plants a healthy start. If needed, lightly water the plants. Allow to dry out and settle in indirect light for a few days.

STAYING ALIVE

Congratulations! You finished your dino world and it looks fantastic! But how do you keep it alive and happy? Each chapter provides care tips for specific plant types. We've intentionally recommended hardy, nonfussy plants, but do hold on to those care tags. If you remember the name of your plant, you can look it up online to troubleshoot any issues with light, air circulation, water, feeding, or maintenance.

Remember, your dino world will change over time. Plants will outgrow their space. You'll need to clean the container. A few plants might die. Do your best, but if you need to replace a neglected plant, it's not the end of the world. Throw the old one in the compost and pick out a fresh one, guilt-free, or transplant what you can save, empty your container, wash any materials you can reuse, compost the old soil, and start over with a new dino world. With all these gorgeous projects to choose from, we hope you will make more than one. Happy planting!

HERDS OF A FEATHER FLOCK TOGETHER

Coelophysis

AT A GLANCE

TIME	225 to 202 million years ago
PLACE	Southwestern United States
ROCKS	Chinle Formation
DINOSAURS	Carnivores (small): *Coelophysis*, *Chindesaurus*, other *Coelophysis*-like dinosaurs, dinosaur cousin *Dromomeron*
CO-STARRING	Ferns, cycads, conifers Freshwater clams Freshwater sharks and lungfish Giant predatory amphibians (*Koskinonodon*) Phytosaurs Aetosaurs Dinosaur-like crocodile relatives Dicynodonts (*Placerias*)
NOTABLE SITES	Arizona: Petrified Forest National Park, Placerias Quarry New Mexico: Ghost Ranch

TIME TRAVEL
TO THE TRIASSIC

Have you ever seen a picture of planet Earth from space? If you could travel back in time to around 220 million years ago and then look down at the American Southwest, you would be in for a surprise. During the Triassic Period, Arizona and New Mexico were near the equator. Talk about a sweaty hike! Walking around, you would have seen very tall conifers that looked quite different from the pines and spruces that we're familiar with today. Ferns and cycads were around, but there were no flowers on the earth.

If you tiptoed very quietly in these Triassic woods, you might have been lucky enough to spot a group of slender *Coelophysis* dinosaurs. One of the earliest known dinosaurs, *Coelophysis* were waist-high and 10 feet long. Watch out near that river! Long-snouted phytosaurs and heavily armored aetosaurs also liked wet areas. These strange creatures were not dinosaurs but early relatives of snapping crocodiles.

Today the Southwest is quite different. If you have ever been to Petrified Forest National Park, you probably saw some of the colorful Triassic-age rocks. These rocks formed in floodplains, lakes, streams, and deserts between about 225 and 200 million years ago. Geologists call these rocks the Chinle Formation, and this geological unit can be seen in many southwestern states, including Arizona, Colorado, Nevada, New Mexico, and Utah. Today's visitors to the rocks of the Chinle Formation will see living cacti and lizards, but no tall conifers, *Coelophysis* dinosaurs, or phytosaurs.

In the American Southwest, *Coelophysis* lived with nondinosaurs such as the fierce phytosaurs and aetosaurs. Can you name any other Triassic dinosaurs? *Plateosaurus* was found in Europe. This

ANCIENT CROCODILES

Phytosaurs looked almost exactly like modern crocodiles and alligators. One difference gives them away: their nostrils were on a small ridge in front of their eyes instead of at the tip of the snout.

WEIRD AMPHIBIAN: *Koskinonodon*

We usually think of amphibians as small animals, but the Chinle streams and lakes were home to *Koskinonodon*, a 10-foot-long predatory amphibian with a long tail and a massive flat head.

TRIASSIC HIPPO: *Placerias*

One of the bigger animals of the Chinle Formation was herbivorous *Placerias*, a hippo-like cousin to modern mammals. Parts of at least forty of these animals have been found in one place near St. Johns, Arizona.

plant eater had a small head but long neck and tail. It was much larger than *Coelophysis*, but not as large as its younger cousins—the giant four-footed herbivores of the Jurassic and Cretaceous, such as *Brachiosaurus* and *Diplodocus*.

The first dinosaurs appeared by 230 million years ago. They were rare until a major extinction at the end of the Triassic, about 200 million years ago. This cleared the way for dinosaurs to thrive. We don't yet know what caused this extinction, or why dinosaurs survived when many other groups didn't. What do you think—why did Triassic dinosaurs survive?

IT WASN'T JUST *COELOPHYSIS*

Coelophysis that were found at Ghost Ranch lived close to the end of the Triassic. Older rocks in the Chinle Formation were deposited when the climate was more humid, but these tropical conditions were coming to an end. The next rocks to be deposited show evidence of huge sandy deserts. Even under a drying climate, there were still many kinds of animals. So far, about a dozen kinds of vertebrates have been found at the *Coelophysis* quarry, including:

SMALL FISH

- *Chinlea,* a freshwater coelacanth related to the rare modern coelacanths found in the deep ocean

- *Vancleavea,* a strange-looking armored reptile that had a tail with a tall fin (like some swimming reptiles today), short limbs, and fang-like teeth

- *Eucoelophysis,* once thought to be related to *Coelophysis* but now known to be a dinosaur cousin that walked on all fours

- *Daemonosaurus,* a small theropod dinosaur with a shorter skull than *Coelophysis* and long, spiky teeth

- *Effigia,* a reptile that looked a lot like ostrich-mimic dinosaurs but was actually related to crocodiles

SMALL CROCODILE RELATIVES THAT COULD WALK ON TWO OR FOUR LEGS

- *Redondasaurus,* a large, crocodile-like phytosaur

- *Drepanosaur,* a small reptile that looked something like a chameleon with a long neck and a birdlike head

- *Whitakersaurus,* related to the living lizard-like tuatara of New Zealand

DID YOU KNOW?

Native Americans in the Southwest frequently used Chinle petrified wood to make tools. Not only is the wood hard, durable, workable, and abundant but it looks pretty too! Dinosaur fossils are uncommon in the Chinle Formation, with one exception: *Coelophysis. Coelophysis* is known from hundreds of skeletons found at Ghost Ranch in New Mexico. This dinosaur was small and carnivorous, and it walked on two legs. It probably used its long, small, sharp teeth and grasping hands to eat small prey. Because many skeletons were found in this one place, scientists believe that *Coelophysis* may have lived in groups or herds.

MISTAKEN IDENTITY

Many Triassic animals have no modern relatives, so when we find partial fossils, it's easy to make mistakes. Some unusual Triassic animals were once mistakenly identified as dinosaurs or pterosaurs.

WHAT IS A THEROPOD ANYWAY?

Coelophysis was an early theropod dinosaur. Almost all of the dinosaurs that ate meat (carnivores) or both plants and meat (omnivores) were theropods, and like *Coelophysis,* they all walked on two legs. Later theropods include dinosaurs such as *Dilophosaurus, Allosaurus, Spinosaurus, Velociraptor,* and *Tyrannosaurus.* Birds are also theropods. Only a few early theropods such as *Coelophysis* are known from fossil bones, but their footprints are found in many places (see chapter 2).

Fallen Log Terrarium

Who wants to build a Triassic landscape for a group of *Coelophysis*? You'll create a fallen log terrarium with some of the coolest plants around. Air plants (*Tillandsia*) suck their nutrients and moisture from the air around them. They come in all sorts of kooky shapes. Look for ones that resemble Triassic plants such as ferns, cycads, and conifers. Remember, paleontologists have evidence that *Coelophysis*—one of the earliest dinosaurs—lived in groups or herds. As you create your design, be sure to leave enough space for your *Coelophysis* family to roam and hide. Did you know that nondinosaur relatives of modern crocodiles and alligators also lived with *Coelophysis*? They are called phytosaurs and aetosaurs. Why not make a river or lake for those creatures too? Watch out, *Coelophysis*! Those snapping phytosaurs get hungry.

TOY TALK

TOP TOY: *Coelophysis*
SUBSTITUTE: a raptor such as a *Velociraptor* or *Deinonychus* (trim off the "killer claws" on the feet for better accuracy)
ADDITIONAL TOYS: phytosaur, aetosaur, or crocodile

MATERIALS & TOOLS

1 container with low sides (shallow tray, jelly roll pan, or 9 x 13-inch glass casserole dish)

Sand, river rock, or aquarium gravel

Live moss or preserved sheet moss

1 small log or piece of wood with nooks and crannies

Blue glass stones

1 Spanish moss (*Tillandsia usneoides*)

1 to 3 additional air plants

Decorations of your choice: rocks, preserved reindeer or pillow moss, sticks, feathers, gemstones, seedpods, beads, marbles, other found objects

2 or 3 dinosaur toys, miniature size

TIP: If you can find live moss (such as haircap moss or cushion moss), it would look lovely in your fallen log terrarium. Just be sure to add a thin layer of potting soil, gently press the live moss into the top of the soil, and keep moist. Spanish moss is an air plant, and it doesn't need soil. Preserved mosses such as sheet moss, reindeer moss, or pillow moss don't need soil either.

DIRECTIONS

1. Create a base layer with sand, river rock, aquarium gravel, or layers of preserved sheet moss. Make mounds or hills as you go. Finish with a layer of live or preserved sheet moss. (Remember to end with a thin layer of potting soil if using live moss.)

2. Set your log into the landscape.

3. Use your blue glass stones to make a river or pond. Drape the log with the Spanish moss or tuck an air plant into its nooks and crannies. Experiment with the remaining air plants, moss, and any other decorations to create your own unique Triassic world.

4. Have fun playing with your herd of *Coelophysis* in their forest world. Just watch out for those chomping phytosaurs and aetosaurs in the water!

PLANT PICKS

Air plants (*Tillandsia*) come in all sorts of weird, spidery shapes and sizes. Since they don't require soil, they are very easy to care for. Check out *Tillandsia funckiana*, which looks like a pine tree. The vibrant air fern (or Neptune plant) isn't actually a *Tillandsia*, but it doesn't need soil. Spanish moss (*Tillandsia usneoides*) looks like a pile of moss, and for a cycad look-alike, check out the many varieties of *Tillandsia ionantha* and *Tillandsia xerographica*.

PLANT DOCTOR:
How To Take Care Of Air Plants (*Tillandsia*)

As their name suggests, air plants suck moisture and nutrients from the air. In the wild, they attach themselves to trees or rocks. They don't need to be planted in soil. However, air plants do need light, good air circulation, and water. Place them near a window so they get bright but indirect sunshine. Make sure they get plenty of fresh air. (Don't put them in a dark corner or enclose them under glass.) Mist them with water several times a week. If you live in a dry climate, you might need to mist every day. Once a week, take all your air plants and soak them for 20 minutes in a bowl of clean, lukewarm water. Allow to dry completely, upside down on a paper towel or rack, before putting them back in their containers. If you're lucky, healthy air plants will sprout babies. Once the baby shoots are big enough, you can gently pinch them off the mother plant and let them grow on their own.

Dragonfly in Amber

Did you know that the dragonfly is one of the oldest creatures on earth? Get ready to preserve toy dragonflies in homemade "amber." Real amber is fossilized tree resin. If you've ever seen amber, you know it has a lovely golden glow. You'll make amber from nontoxic clear glue (it must be clear, or your amber won't be see-through) and food dye. These creations make beautiful paperweights and unique gifts. Hold one of your dragonflies in amber up to a window. See how it catches the light? Isn't that gorgeous?

MATERIALS & TOOLS

Flexible molds that fit your dragonflies (recycled plastic lids, silicone muffin tins or regular well-greased muffin tins, silicone candy molds, or cookie cutters set on parchment or wax paper)

Neutral cooking oil or Vaseline

1 (5-ounce) container nontoxic clear glue

Red and yellow food dye

Gold glitter (optional)

2 or 3 small toy dragonflies

DIRECTIONS

1. Grease your molds generously with the oil or Vaseline, making sure to reach all nooks and crannies.

2. Open the container of glue and carefully add 2 drops of red food dye and 6 drops of yellow. Shake the bottle. It doesn't matter if the color isn't completely incorporated. Add a tiny amount of glitter, if desired. You should have a swirl of transparent, orangey-amber color. If needed, add another drop of either yellow or red. Put the cap back on the glue.

3. Place 1 dragonfly in each of your molds. Drizzle the glue over and around each dragonfly. The more glue you use, the longer it will take to dry. Use the smallest amount possible!

4. Allow to dry until firm. (Remember, this can take as long as a week.) Carefully pop your creations out of the molds. If they're still tacky, flip upside down on a greased plate (or piece of wax paper) and allow to harden completely.

TIP: Plan on at least a week of drying time, depending on the size of your mold.

CH. 2

TRACKS
Behavior but No Bones

AT A GLANCE

TIME	202 to 174 million years ago
PLACE	Southwestern United States
ROCKS	Navajo Sandstone Kayenta Formation Moenave Formation/Wingate Sandstone
DINOSAURS	Carnivores (small): *Segisaurus* Carnivores (medium): *Dilophosaurus* Herbivores (small): *Scutellosaurus* Herbivores (medium): *Seitaad*
FOSSIL TRACKS	*Grallator* *Eubrontes*
CO-STARRING	Microbial mats Horsetails, conifers Spiders and scorpions (tracks) Small terrestrial crocodile relatives (bones and tracks) Early mammal relatives (bones, tracks, and burrows)
NOTABLE SITES	Arizona: The Wave Utah: Glen Canyon National Recreation Area, Zion National Park

DINOSAUR DETECTIVE: HOW TRACKS LEAVE CLUES BEHIND

The great fictional detective Sherlock Holmes often used footprints to solve crimes. In a similar way, paleontologists examine fossilized footprints to help reconstruct ancient scenes from the past. Did you know that some dinosaur tracks became fossilized? Some fossil tracks are very obvious and look as if a dinosaur walked across the landscape last year. Others are difficult to recognize and must be identified by a paleontologist who studies fossil footprints. Fossil footprints belong to a special group of fossils called trace fossils because they reveal what an animal was doing. Other trace fossils include fossil burrows and coprolites (fossil dung).

Fossil tracks are particularly important in ancient rocks in which fossil bones are rare. For example, we haven't found many fossil bones in certain dramatic rocks deposited in the American Southwest in the Early Jurassic. Around 190 million years ago, giant sand dunes covered the area that's now known as the Four Corners region (Arizona, Colorado, New Mexico, and Utah). At that time the area probably looked a lot like the modern-day Sahara. Beds of sand piled up over millions of years and eventually hardened into stone. Sometimes between the dune deposits we find fine-grained beds that represent wetter locations, such as ponds or oases.

Warm, dry conditions lasted throughout much of the Jurassic in western North America, so there are several different geologic formations that represent desert or semiarid environments. The most famous is the Navajo Sandstone, well known for amazing landscapes such as the Wave in Arizona and Checkerboard Mesa in Utah.

Even though the climate in the Jurassic dunes was harsh, there was still plenty of life in those ancient deserts. Because fossil bones are rare in dune sediments, paleontologists have mostly learned about the animals that lived there from their tracks. Fossilized scorpion tracks and insect burrows tell us about some of the smaller creatures that scurried across the dunes or hid in the sand. Ancient lizard-like animals, crocodilians, mammal relatives, and several kinds of dinosaurs also left fossil footprints. Some large burrows may have been made by the ancient mammal relatives. Rare body fossils from the ancient dune sediments help put some faces to the fossil footprints. For example, large theropod tracks were probably made by the crested *Dilophosaurus* or other similar large carnivorous dinosaurs. Partial skeletons of smaller theropods, prosauropods, and crocodile and mammal relatives point to other possible track makers.

Tracks are unique because they show what a living animal was doing, unlike a body fossil, which represents a dead animal. Like Sherlock Holmes, modern dinosaur detectives can learn many things from fossil footprints:

- A set of tracks can show how fast a dinosaur was moving when it made the footprints.

- Well-preserved tracks can show details of the feet, such as pads and scales.

- Trackways can show the posture of a dinosaur.

- Tracks provide direct evidence of behavior and can show if dinosaurs traveled in groups.

When you think of a paleontologist, you probably imagine someone digging up bones. But tracks are just as important as bones because they help us understand how dinosaurs lived and died.

BURROWS

The Navajo Sandstone preserves fossil burrows as well as fossil tracks. One kind is approximately 5 to 10 inches in diameter and has been found in large complicated networks in rocks that formed between dunes. This kind of burrow may have been dug by small mammal relatives that lived in groups, similar to voles or mole rats. Much larger, simple burrows—more than 12 inches across and 8 inches high—may be dwelling shelters dug by larger mammal relatives.

STROMATOLITES

Stromatolites are layered fossils left by growing microbial mats. They most commonly form in harsh aquatic environments, such as tidal flats and desert ponds. Some more than 15 feet tall have been found in Navajo Sandstone rocks of Capitol Reef National Park, Utah.

DESERT LAKE?

Near St. George, Utah, rocks from the beginning of the Jurassic show a large, salty lake with fish bones and dinosaur tracks. Carnivorous dinosaurs probably caught and scavenged fish there.

EARLY JURASSIC DINOSAUR TRACK MAKERS

The dinosaurs that made the dune tracks included several kinds of large and small theropod dinosaurs, prosauropods (cousins to the giant sauropods that appeared later in time), and small, herbivorous dinosaurs with beaks. It's very difficult to attach a kind of track to a specific kind of skeleton, so there's a separate naming system for tracks. For example, two of the most common types of tracks in these rocks are called *Grallator* and *Eubrontes*. *Grallator* refers to small three-toed theropod tracks, around 2 to 6 inches long, and *Eubrontes* is used for larger theropod tracks, around 10 to 20 inches long.

IF YOU FIND A FOSSIL . . .

Rocks with dinosaur tracks have been found around the top of Lake Powell in Glen Canyon National Recreation Area. Hidden dinosaur tracks can also appear when the water recedes. If you find a fossil in a national park, don't disturb it! Take pictures and tell a ranger about it instead.

BIRDS?

When dinosaur tracks were first found, in New England in the early 1800s, they were thought to be the tracks of large birds. We now know that birds are dinosaurs, so this wasn't a bad guess!

Sand Ribbons Terrarium

Imagine you're walking in a dry, swirling desert. All around you, piles of colored sand form towering dunes. Critters scramble over the sand. Small mammals dig under the surface, leaving burrows behind. This layered sand terrarium is more than just a desert scene—it features hardened dinosaur tracks. If you don't have time to make the baked dino tracks, grab one of your dinosaur toys and make impressions in the sand with its feet. Be sure to mist the top of the sand with water first so you can really see the outline of the tracks.

Air plants (*Tillandsia*) make a striking addition to this terrarium. Part of the epiphyte family of plants, air plants don't need soil—simply rest them on top of the sand. (See "Plant Doctor," page 6, for ways to keep your air plants healthy.) Add a sparkly geode, a crystal, or a small piece of wood. This project looks complicated, but it's actually super easy. Invite some friends over, turn on some music, and get ready to make some sand art.

MATERIALS & TOOLS

1 clear, tall container (glass or clear hard plastic with high sides)

Disposable piping bags, funnel, scoop, or spoon

Colored Sand in several shades (see page 50 for activity)

White decorative sand

Plain play sand

Baked Tracks (see page 19 for activity)

1 or 2 air plants

Decorations of your choice: glittery geodes, small crystals, rocks, sticks

Sand tray tools such as a miniature rake, dry paintbrush, or popsicle stick (optional)

TIP: If you live near the ocean, feel free to replace the white decorative sand and play sand with beach sand!

DIRECTIONS

1. If you plan to use the piping bags, fill them with colored and white sand and cinch the openings with rubber bands. Set them on a tray (to keep sand from spilling everywhere). Snip the tips just before starting. If you prefer, you could also set out bowls of sand, and use a scoop, funnel, spoon, or even just your hands.

2. Pour colored sand around the edges of the terrarium. Sandwiching the colors with layers of white will make the design pop.

3. Build layers and hills around the edge of the container, one color at a time. As you go, fill the center of the terrarium with plain play sand. (Just use a scoop for the plain play sand since you'll need a lot to fill up the center of the container.) Keep checking your design from the side. You'll see waves and ribbons of color start to form. Make the layers as thick or thin as you like. Finish with a thick layer of white decorative sand or plain play sand.

4. Set your baked dinosaur tracks on top of the sand. Add an air plant or two, a crystal or geode, some sticks or rocks, or any other found objects that you like.

5. Try sprinkling sand on top of your tracks. Then have fun brushing your tracks clean with a paintbrush or digging them out with a popsicle stick. Use a miniature rake to scratch designs in the sand.

COLORED SAND

Colored sand is available at craft stores such as Michaels, but it can be expensive. Using colored sand just around the edges (where people will actually see it) saves on materials. (If you have enough colored sand, it's perfectly fine to ditch the play-sand center.) Did you know you can easily make colored "sand" at home? (It's actually made from salt—see "Colored Sand," page 50, for the recipe.) Just be sure if you're using air plants that you end with a thick layer of real sand. Salt kills air plants. *No bueno.*

SAND DESIGN TIPS: SUNSETS AND BURROWS

Layers of yellow, orange, and pink or red make a vibrant sunset. Or what about a layer of blue sand for the ocean, or green for plants? To make a bird, sprinkle in a layer of blue (for sky) or white (for clouds). Then create the shape of bird wings. Add a short, thin layer of black sand on top. Using a chopstick or skewer, poke down just a little bit into the middle of the black line. It's a bird! To form a burrow, cut an extra-large straw into pieces and press one open end against the edge of your container. Bury it in the sand and imagine all the strange critters that would use it as a passageway.

Baked Tracks

Have you ever seen homemade Christmas tree ornaments or handprints? They were probably made out of salt dough. Why not whip up a batch? You'll roll it out to create a set of dinosaur tracks. You can use salt dough for lots of projects in this book. Tint it blue to create a pond or river shape. Keep it plain white and shape it into an ammonite (see "Salt Dough Ammonite," page 29). Here, we will use salt dough to stamp dinosaur tracks. Warning: this dough may look like yummy sugar cookie dough, but it tastes horrible!

MATERIALS & TOOLS

1 cup table salt

2 cups flour, plus a little extra, for dusting

¾ cup water

Rolling pin

Toy dinosaurs, miniature size

Round or oval cookie cutter or knife

Baking sheet

Parchment paper

Nontoxic paint, glitter, or other decorations (optional)

DIRECTIONS

1. Stir together the salt and flour in a large mixing bowl. Add the water a little bit at a time, just until it starts to come together to form a stiff dough. (You may not need all the water, or you may need a bit more.)

2. Turn the dough onto a floured surface. Use your hands to knead the dough until it's smooth and no longer sticky. It should feel like play dough.

3. Dust your rolling pin and surface with flour. Roll out the dough until it's about ¼-inch thick. Use your dinosaur toys to make track impressions. Cut out the tracks using a cookie cutter or a knife.

4. Place your tracks on a baking sheet lined with parchment paper and allow to dry for about 24 hours. Carefully flip your tracks halfway through so that both sides get nice and firm. Or, if you live in a humid climate, ask a grown-up to help you bake your creations at 250°F for about 1 hour, or until dry and hard.

5. Leave the tracks plain or embellish with paint, glitter, or other decorations of your choice.

ORNAMENTS & NECKLACES

These tracks make awesome ornaments or jewelry. Before drying, punch a small hole near the top of the design. Check the hole halfway through drying. If it's sealing up, carefully repunch the hole and continue drying. Once your creation is hard, thread some yarn or a ribbon through the hole. Look what you made! Hang it on a tree, string it onto a necklace, or suspend it in a window.

MMM . . . THAT SMELLS GOOD

For extra special salt dough creations, why not add a fragrance? For a Valentine's Day gift, try adding dried rose petals, a couple drops of red food dye, and a few drops of rose essential oil. Pine needle oil makes you feel like you're walking in the woods, vanilla and cinnamon remind everyone of warm cookies, and citrus peel smells like sunshine.

UNDER THE SEA
Plesiosaurus

AT A GLANCE

TIME	200 to 180 million years ago
PLACE	Southern England
ROCKS	Lias Group
MARINE REPTILES	*Ichthyosaurus, Plesiosaurus*
DINOSAURS	None (although sometimes dinosaur carcasses washed out to sea)
CO-STARRING	Clams Squid-like ammonites, nautiloids, belemnites Crinoids (sea lilies) Sharks Bony fish Pterosaurs
NOTABLE SITES	Jurassic Coast of Dorset

GIANT REPTILES OF JURASSIC SEAS

Imagine swimming in the Early Jurassic ocean around 200 million years ago. You would have shared the sea with large swimming shellfish and fearsome-looking large marine reptiles. Some of these animals might have viewed you as lunch. Watch out!

Geological studies have shown that in the Early Jurassic, much of Europe was submerged by a shallow sea. Sediments deposited at the bottom of that ancient ocean are now exposed in southern England in fossil-rich limestone rocks known as the Lias. The most common fossils are from invertebrates—animals that lack backbones. Jurassic invertebrates included ammonites, tentacled shellfish that lived in coiled shells with prominent ridges. These extinct animals didn't just sit on the seafloor. They swam through water with jet propulsion. In the Early Jurassic, ammonite shells grew to more than a foot across, but later Cretaceous ammonites were sometimes up to 6 feet in diameter. Clams, snails, and feathery crinoids also lived in the Lias seas.

Swimming alongside the invertebrates were numerous types of sharks and bony fishes. Many of these fish may have resembled modern-day fish. However, the scariest Jurassic animals in the Jurassic seas were different types of toothy marine reptiles. Two well-known types of marine reptiles are ichthyosaurs and plesiosaurs.

Ichthyosaurs looked a bit like modern dolphins, but their tails give them away: dolphin tails are horizontal and move up and down, but ichthyosaur tails were vertical and moved side to side like fish tails. But ichthyosaurs were *reptiles*—they were neither mammals nor fish! Ichthyosaurs often had enormous eyes and long, thin snouts that held many sharp-pointed teeth. Most ichthyosaurs were about 5 to 15 feet long, but the largest reached 50 to 70 feet long.

Plesiosaurs were the other main group of marine reptiles in the ancient Lias seas. They didn't look much like anything alive today. They had broad bodies with short tails, and their four limbs had evolved into flippers. Plesiosaurs with long necks and small heads probably caught small prey, while plesiosaurs with large heads and short necks probably went after other marine reptiles. The biggest plesiosaurs belonged to this second group, and some from the Late Jurassic may have been more than 30 feet long and weighed 10 to 20 tons.

Ichthyosaurs and plesiosaurs were not really dinosaurs, but they swam in the oceans at the same time that dinosaurs stomped around on land. Like the big dinosaurs, ichthyosaurs and plesiosaurs are now extinct. However, their fossils remind us that many different kinds of animals have made their home in the sea throughout Earth history. Remember that about 70 percent of Earth is covered by seawater! We're lucky that fossils can tell us what kinds of creatures lived in the ocean millions of years ago. Since we know that giant marine reptiles lived in the Lias seas, perhaps a visit to the Jurassic ocean would have best been undertaken in a submarine.

CAN YOU GUESS?

Question: **What are some examples of marine reptiles living today?**
Answer: **Sea turtles, saltwater crocodiles, marine iguanas, and sea snakes are all living marine reptiles.**

FLOATING CARCASSES

Dinosaurs were not marine animals, but sometimes their carcasses floated to sea. Some of the best English dinosaur fossils were preserved when *Scelidosaurus* (an early armored dinosaur) carcasses were washed out to sea and buried in marine sediment.

WATER BABIES

Unlike most reptiles, ichthyosaurs and plesiosaurs didn't lay eggs. They gave birth, without eggs, in the water, as whales do today.

NECK OR TAIL?

Nobody had ever seen a neck as long as the neck of the American plesiosaur *Elasmosaurus* when the scientist Edward Drinker Cope described it in 1869. In fact, Cope thought the neck was the tail, and drew *Elasmosaurus* with the head on the wrong end! When his mistake was discovered by a rival paleontologist, his embarrassment helped to set off the "Bone Wars" (see page 35).

SWIMMING LESSONS

Unlike many marine animals, which use their tails to swim, plesiosaurs relied on their four flippers for power. Plesiosaurs combined the motions of both front and back flippers to get more power than relying on one pair alone.

MARINE REPTILES

Many kinds of reptiles evolved to live in salt water. In addition to ichthyosaurs and plesiosaurs, there were several other types of marine reptiles that are now extinct too. Some of those marine reptiles may have ventured onto land. However, the fins of ichthyosaurs and plesiosaurs were so well adapted to swimming that they probably spent their entire lives in the ocean. Some examples of marine reptiles include:

- Placodonts lived during the Triassic. The first placodonts looked like marine iguanas, but they evolved much broader bodies and eventually looked more like turtles. They had hard, flat teeth for eating shellfish.

- Nothosaurs also lived in the Triassic and looked a bit like skinny, long-necked plesiosaurs. However, they had hands and feet instead of true paddles. They may have lived like seals.

- *Shastasaurus sikanniensis,* the biggest known marine reptile, may have reached 70 feet long and weighed nearly 70 tons. It lived in the Late Triassic of British Columbia.

- Mosasaurs appeared in the Cretaceous and their fossils are common in rocks from shallow continental seas. They may have taken over the predatory role of ichthyosaurs, which dwindled during the Cretaceous. Mosasaur bodies were built like giant lizards with flippers.

Underwater Terrarium

Water, water everywhere! Wouldn't it be amazing to swim with ancient sea creatures? The prehistoric underwater world was like nothing you've ever seen. What makes this habitat extra special is that you get to use aquatic plants. That's right, you'll be using plants that get their nutrients straight from the water rather than soil. Have fun picking out a floating hydrophyte with feathery, kelp-like roots. Or choose a lime-green marimo moss ball and watch it bob around in the water. Admire your underwater world from the side. What about a piece of coral, some shells, or driftwood? Have fun making a splash with your *Plesiosaurus* and other marine reptiles. Let's dive in!

TOY TALK

TOP TOY: *Plesiosaurus*
SUBSTITUTES: *Ichthyosaurus, Elasmosaurus,* or *Attenborosaurus*
ADDITIONAL TOYS: Other marine reptiles from a prehistoric sea life bucket or tube

TIP: To dechlorinate tap water, assemble your terrarium but stop before you add the plants. Leave the terrarium (uncovered) for 24 hours. The chlorine will evaporate. Then add your plants.

MATERIALS & TOOLS

1 clear container (tall cylinder, bubble terrarium, small aquarium tank, apothecary jar, or a fish bowl)

Aquarium gravel or shale, rinsed

Decorations of your choice: sea glass, shells, coral, driftwood, sand dollars, colored rocks

Toy marine reptiles, miniature size

Dechlorinated water

1 to 3 marimo moss balls or other floating aquatic plants (see "Plant Picks" and "No Soil Required," page 27)

DIRECTIONS

1. For this project, your container and materials must be sparkling clean. Wash your container and all large materials. Rinse the gravel in a colander or sieve until the water runs clear. Tap water is fine for this step.

2. Place a thin layer of gravel into your container. Arrange your ocean floor decorations, using your imagination to create your own watery underworld. Add your *Plesiosaurus* and other marine reptiles. Make little nooks for creatures to hide.

3. Slowly fill the container with room temperature, dechlorinated water, leaving a few inches of space at the top. Add your marimo moss ball or other floating aquatic plants. Check out your creation from the side.

4. Follow the directions for light requirements and care that came with your chosen plants. About twice a month, you'll need to replace the water with fresh dechlorinated water. (Use a siphon tube—a long flexible tube found in hardware stores—to make it easy.)

NO SOIL REQUIRED

Hydrophytes (also called aquatic plants) are plants that grow in water. Just like plants that live on land, hydrophytes need light. Unlike regular plants, they draw nutrients from the water. Oxygenating aquatics such as Java moss (*Vesicularia dubyana*) thrive submerged under the water. Pickerel rush (*Pontederia cordata*) and yellow flag iris (*Iris pseudacorus*) are examples of bog or shallow water aquatics; they flourish halfway out of the water. Floating aquatics, such as water lily (*Nymphaea*) and sacred lotus (*Nelumbo nucifera*), have deep roots but their leaves rest on the surface.

PLANT PICKS

For this terrarium, marimo moss balls are the best choice. Marimo moss balls aren't moss but algae, and yes, they're alive! In the wild, they live in cool lakes. (*Marimo* means "seaweed ball" in Japanese.) Keep them in low indirect light, and replace the water with fresh dechlorinated water twice a month. Marimo moss balls grow very slowly. They look like fluorescent sea creatures bobbing in the water. How cool is that? Find them in the aquarium section of your local pet store.

If you can't find marimo moss balls, other floating aquatics, such as water lettuce or water hyacinth, will also work. (Avoid true aquatics or semiaquatics because they're very difficult to maintain without a filter or fish to control algae bloom.) You can also try a philodendron cutting instead. A common houseplant, philodendron thrives on neglect and grows like a weed. Maybe you have one in your house right now. If so, take a cutting from the philodendron and submerge the stem in water (leaving the upper leaves exposed). While not a true aquatic, philodendron cuttings will grow quite happily in water. Reap all the healthy benefits of air-cleansing, mood-boosting green plants but ditch the weekly watering. Sounds like a win!

Salt Dough Ammonite

Ammonites are prehistoric shells of creatures that lived in the oceans 400 to 66 million years ago. The term *ammonite* comes from the spiral shape of the fossils. Ancient Romans thought they resembled the ram's horns of the ancient Egyptian god Ammon. Ammonites are related to modern-day octopuses and squids. They went extinct at the same time as the giant dinosaurs of the Mesozoic, leaving behind cool fossils.

MATERIALS & TOOLS

Salt Dough (see page 19 for recipe)

Fork, toothpick, or butter knife

Pencil

Cookie sheet

Parchment paper

Paint, paintbrush, glitter (optional)

DIRECTIONS

1. Take a piece of salt dough and roll it into a long, thin sausage shape.

2. Using the side of a fork, toothpick, or butter knife (make sure a grown-up is with you!), press small slits into the top of the snake you've made. As you get closer to the other end of your sausage shape, you can switch to using the side of a pencil. This will make bigger impressions.

3. Starting on the end with the fork marks, gently curl one end up until you have a tight spiral shape. Try not to mash the tube or you'll lose the impressions you made. (If you brush the inner curve with water before starting to curl, it will stick together better.)

4. Line a cookie sheet with parchment paper (or grease lightly). Place your ammonites on the sheet, leaving at least an inch of space between them.

5. There are two ways to harden and dry out your ammonite.

   - Option 1: Bake your ammonite. Have an adult help you. Preheat the oven to 250°F. Bake for 1 to 2 hours, or until dry and hard. The baking time will depend on the thickness of your ammonite.

   - Option 2: Skip the oven. Instead, simply allow the ammonite to dry out at room temperature. This could take up to several days, depending on your climate and the thickness of your ammonite. Flip to dry out the underside. When your ammonite is hard and dry, it's ready!

6. Decorate your ammonite with paint or glitter, or leave it plain.

CRETACEOUS CHARMS

In the western United States, there are fossils of a Cretaceous straight-shelled ammonite called *Baculites.* The shells often disintegrate into segments representing the chambers. The walls separating the chambers have complex patterns that make the pieces look something like small animal figurines. Sometimes Native Americans would pick up these segments to use as charms (*iniskim,* or "buffalo stones") because of the shapes.

MARY ANNING

Mary Anning was a famous paleontologist who lived in England in the 1800s. At that time, the field of paleontology was brand-new. Mary Anning began collecting fossils with her family when she was very young. In fact, she helped discover one of the first ichthyosaur skeletons when she was only about 11 years old! Mary Anning discovered many other important fossils in the Lias, including the first plesiosaur skeletons and an early pterosaur. She didn't always receive the credit she deserved for her discoveries. She was a woman of low social standing at a time when aristocratic white men dominated the scientific world. However, Mary Anning did receive more honor for her achievements later in her life. Today, most paleontologists recognize and appreciate Mary Anning's important contributions to the science of paleontology.

JURASSIC GIANTS

Stegosaurus, Allosaurus, and Apatosaurus

AT A GLANCE

TIME	156 to 146 million years ago
PLACE	Western United States, from Montana south to New Mexico
ROCKS	Morrison Formation
DINOSAURS	Carnivores (small): *Coelurus, Ornitholestes* Carnivores (large): *Allosaurus, Ceratosaurus, Torvosaurus* Herbivores (small): *Dryosaurus, Gargoyleosaurus, Othnielosaurus* Herbivores (medium): *Camptosaurus, Stegosaurus* Herbivores (large): *Apatosaurus, Barosaurus, Brachiosaurus, Camarasaurus, Diplodocus, Supersaurus*
CO-STARRING	Ferns, ginkgoes, conifers Freshwater clams Turtles Terrestrial and aquatic crocodile cousins Pterosaurs Early mammals and mammal cousins
NOTABLE SITES	Colorado: Dry Mesa, Fruita, Garden Park Utah: Cleveland-Lloyd Dinosaur Quarry, Dinosaur National Monument Wyoming: Bone Cabin, Como Bluff

ROUND UP THE USUAL SUSPECTS

Stegosaurus! Apatosaurus! Allosaurus! Many of us recognize images of these classic dinosaurs from movies, cartoons, and toy stores. Did you know that these dinosaurs have something in common? They were all found in the Morrison Formation of the western United States. The Morrison Formation is one of the most famous dinosaur-producing rock formations in the world. (To see a recreation of the Morrison Foundation, see "Utah Dinosaur Dig," page 101.) Like the Chinle Formation discussed in chapter 1, the Morrison Formation is made up of colorful rocks deposited in floodplains, lakes, and streams. However, the Morrison Formation is much younger, dating to 156 to 146 million years ago. At that time, dinosaurs were the dominant animals that lived on land. Dinosaur fossils have been found in the Morrison Formation from Montana to Oklahoma and New Mexico. By far the best fossils have been found in Colorado, Utah, and Wyoming.

If you went back to the time of the Morrison Formation, it would have looked quite unfamiliar. As in the earlier Triassic Period, flowering plants were absent or were so rare that we have no fossil record for them. There were no broadleaf trees, no flowering shrubs, and no grasses. What plants were around? Tall conifers, ginkgo trees, and tree ferns shaded the land, and cycads, ferns, and horsetails made up the ground cover. Although there were no grasses, large fields of ferns probably resembled "fern savannas." But the biggest difference between the Triassic and the Jurassic was that enormous dinosaurs moved across the landscape. This was a time of giants.

The largest dinosaurs in the Morrison Formation were the long-necked sauropods. Sauropods in the Morrison Formation are well known. You probably know many of their names: *Brachiosaurus* had long arms and a sloping back; *Barosaurus* had a very long neck; *Camarasaurus* had a boxy skull; and *Apatosaurus* and *Diplodocus* are probably the most familiar of all. Each of these animals could reach lengths of more than 70 feet and weigh more than 10 tons! The biggest of the big may have been more than 100 feet long and 30 tons in weight.

Not all of the Morrison dinosaurs were large. Some were very small, such as 3-foot-long *Fruitadens* that had fang-like teeth in its lower jaw. Plant-eating beaked dinosaurs came in several sizes, from large *Camptosaurus*, to medium-sized *Dryosaurus* (about the weight of an adult human), to small *Othnielosaurus*. Slow, heavy dinosaurs also foraged for plants, including the familiar plate-backed *Stegosaurus* and at least two kinds of armored dinosaurs. These plant eaters were hunted by carnivorous theropod dinosaurs. The largest meat eaters, such as *Torvosaurus*, were only a little smaller than *Tyrannosaurus*. *Allosaurus* was the most common and could be more than 30 feet long. Somewhat smaller was *Ceratosaurus*, known for its nose horn.

Tiny fossil bones tell us that many smaller animals were also present. True frogs and salamanders lived near water, where lungfish and bony fish swam. Turtles and ancient crocodile relatives were common. Lizards and many small rodent-like mammals also skittered about while several kinds of pterosaurs flew overhead. These smaller animals played important roles in the Jurassic ecosystem, but they had to keep out of the way of the huge dinosaurs that dominated the landscape.

WEIRD BUT TRUE

One of the strangest Morrison mammals is *Fruitafossor* from Colorado. It was tiny (weighing maybe 5 grams) and built for digging into termite nests and eating the insects.

CAN YOU GUESS?

Question: What do Colorado, Portugal, and Tanzania have in common?

Answer: Many of the same dinosaurs found in the Morrison Formation, or their close cousins, are found in rocks of the same age in Portugal and Tanzania. The supercontinent Pangaea was breaking up in the Jurassic, but dinosaurs were still similar across the continents.

MISSING BONE

In 1878, Edward Drinker Cope named *Amphicoelias fragillimus,* possibly the biggest known dinosaur, from a partial backbone found in the Morrison Formation of Colorado. The backbone may have belonged to an animal close to 200 feet long and weighing more than 120 tons. However, only the description remains; the bone was either lost or fell apart, so we have no way of checking the report.

BONE WARS

Many of the fossils and famous species of dinosaurs from the Morrison Formation were described during the late nineteenth century. During this time, paleontologists Edward Drinker Cope and Othniel Charles Marsh were locked in a rivalry sometimes called the "Bone Wars." They were racing to name as many fossils as they could, because the rules of naming organisms give priority to the first assigned name. For example, Marsh and Cope both described fossils of our familiar plated dinosaur, but Marsh's name *Stegosaurus* beat Cope's *Hypsirhophus.* In the case of *Allosaurus,* Marsh also won, beating Cope's *Epanterias.* Poor Cope! Nobody remembers his old names for *Stegosaurus* and *Allosaurus.*

BATTLE: *ALLOSAURUS* VERSUS *STEGOSAURUS*

Even though *Stegosaurus* was slow, it would have been dangerous prey for an *Allosaurus.* A large *Stegosaurus* might have been 20 to 30 feet long and weighed 2 to 3 tons, making it similar in size to an *Allosaurus.* Although the thin plates were probably not primarily for defense, the spikes on the end of the tail could have been used against predators. A *Stegosaurus* tail had four spikes, two pointing to the left and two to the right, each up to 3 feet long. If a *Stegosaurus* spotted an *Allosaurus* before it could attack, the herbivore could turn to keep its spikes between it and the predator. The *Allosaurus* could then either keep moving and watch for an opening or try to find easier prey. *Allosaurus* had sharp teeth and powerful arms that could have been used for grappling with prey. Fossilized evidence of predator attacks is rare, but at least three examples show that *Allosaurus* fought *Stegosaurus.* One is a *Stegosaurus* neck plate that appears to have an *Allosaurus* bite mark. We also have evidence that *Stegosaurus* fought back: two *Allosaurus* bones, a tail bone and a hip bone, have damage that match *Stegasaurus* tail spikes.

MILLIONAIRE DONATION: *DIPLODOCUS CARNEGII*

Americans are very familiar with *Brontosaurus,* but in Europe *Diplodocus* is more famous. This is because industrialist and philanthropist Andrew Carnegie donated cast replicas of the mostly complete skeleton of *Diplodocus carnegii* to European museums in the early 1900s.

Box Terrarium

The Morrison Formation is chock-full of dinosaurs we all know and love. Let's build a unique terrarium for these giant dinosaurs using a box of your choice. You can find box planters that come ready to go with a plastic lining, or you can make your own (see "Make a Box Planter," page 39)! Vintage crates, wooden office supply organizers, wicker baskets, and decorative trays all make eye-catching containers. Keep your eye out for interesting shapes and sizes. Just be sure to choose a container with plenty of room for your Jurassic giants to roam and hunt.

TOY TALK

TOP TOYS: *Allosaurus, Stegosaurus, Apatosaurus*

MATERIALS & TOOLS

1 wooden or hard plastic box with plastic lining

Pea gravel, aquarium gravel, or small pebbles

Activated charcoal

Potting soil

3 or 5 plants of your choice

Decorations of your choice: rocks, preserved reindeer or pillow moss, sticks, feathers, gemstones, seedpods, beads, sea glass, colored stones, marbles, other found objects

Chopstick or spoon

Toy dinosaur(s), miniature size

DIRECTIONS

1. Pour a layer of pea gravel or pebbles into the box. This is your drainage layer. Use a spoon to sprinkle a thin layer of activated charcoal over the gravel. (See "Layer Cake Method," page xxii, for more details.)

2. Add a thin layer of potting soil, leaving spaces to dig in your plants. Odd numbers create balance in both nature and design so a grouping of 3 or 5 plants works best. Place your plants, then add more potting soil up to the base of each plant. Use your fingers to gently press the potting soil around the roots of each plant.

3. Add any decorations of your choice, using a chopstick or spoon as a tool. What about a river or pond out of sea glass or blue stones? What about a nest with tiny colored beads as eggs?

4. Position your toy dinosaurs and make this world entirely your own!

WHAT'S IN A NAME?
BRONTOSAURUS

One of Marsh's most famous dinosaurs is *Brontosaurus*, but this name has long been controversial. Marsh named *Brontosaurus* in 1879, but in 1877 he had named another dinosaur *Apatosaurus*. In 1903, another paleontologist, Elmer S. Riggs, concluded that *Brontosaurus* was just a young *Apatosaurus*, and because *Apatosaurus* was the older name, it had priority. However, scientists exhibiting a skeleton in the American Museum of Natural History in New York didn't agree, so they used *Brontosaurus*, and the name spread to the public. Most scientists have preferred to follow Riggs and use *Apatosaurus*, but in 2015 paleontologists made a strong case that *Brontosaurus* is a different species than *Apatosaurus*.

UNSOLVED MYSTERY

The Cleveland-Lloyd Dinosaur Quarry in Utah is one of the most famous dinosaur bonebeds in North America. It's unusual because carnivore remains are more common than herbivore remains: bones from at least 44 *Allosaurus* make up about two-thirds of the dinosaur fossils there. Paleontologists aren't sure how this concentration came to be. What do you think?

MAKE A BOX PLANTER

Set your chosen box on a sturdy surface. Make sure to choose a box that's made from wood, hard plastic, or another durable material (avoid cardboard, which will fall apart after a few waterings). To make a liner, take a heavy-duty trash bag and set it inside your box. Cut out a larger piece than what you think you'll need. Place it inside the container, opening the edges of the piece of plastic over the sides of the box and smoothing out any obvious wrinkles. Staple, nail, or glue the plastic to the upper inside edge of your box. Trim away any excess plastic. Time to start planting!

PLANT PICKS

Moving from the Triassic to the Jurassic, there wasn't a huge difference in plant variety. Choose miniature plants that resemble ferns, mosses, club mosses, horsetails, ginkgoes, cycads, and conifers. (For excellent prehistoric look-alikes, see "Modern Plant Look-Alikes," page xxi.) And remember, no flowering plants or grasses yet!

Designer Dinos

Did you know that you can change your dinosaur toys to make them look more unique? None of your friends will have toy dinosaurs that look quite like yours! Try painting a wound or some blood on your *Stegosaurus* to make your battleground box terrarium more lifelike. What about using markers to draw parasites, worms, or other tiny scavengers on your dino carcass? You could add a crest of feathers, turn your dinosaur into a "mummy" (turn to chapter 8 for more on this!), or sprinkle your dinosaur with glitter.

HERE ARE SOME IDEAS OF MATERIALS TO EXPERIMENT WITH:

Glue

Glitter

Feathers

Scissors

Paint

Paintbrush

Markers

Strips of fabric or paper

Ribbon

Yarn

Pipe cleaners

Rubber bands

Construction paper

DOWN BY THE SEASHORE

Tapejara Takes to the Skies

AT A GLANCE

TIME	100 million years ago
PLACE	Northeastern Brazil
ROCKS	Santana Formation
PTEROSAURS	Fishers: *Anhanguera, Tropeognathus* Herbivores/fruit eaters: *Tapejara* Stork-like land hunters: *Thalassodromeus, Tupuxuara*
DINOSAURS	Carnivores (small): *Mirischia, Santanaraptor* Carnivores (large): *Irritator*
CO-STARRING	Crustaceans Sharks, rays Coelacanths Bony fish

IS A PTEROSAUR A DINOSAUR?

When you dream of summer vacation, what comes to mind? You might imagine yourself at the beach, soaking up sunshine, collecting seashells, and playing all day in the ocean waves. Well, guess what? Tropical beaches were also popular spots for some dinosaurs. But dinosaurs didn't get tans or build sandcastles—they spent their time looking for food or simply walking along the coast as they went from place to place. And dinosaurs weren't alone at the seashore. They had plenty of company in the form of flying pterosaurs and many smaller critters.

For this chapter, we're heading south to northeastern Brazil around 100 million years ago in the middle part of the Cretaceous Period. At that time, a shallow sea covered parts of South America and lagoons formed along the coasts. Those lagoons collected the remains of many plants and animals that lived on this tropical coast, and the sedimentary deposits preserved many of them beautifully. Today, those rocks are called the Santana Formation.

The Santana Formation is special because it preserves a variety of ancient animals. Everything from sharks and rays to clams, snails, and shrimp were at home in the shallow seas. Turtles and crocodiles probably spent time both in the sea and on land. There were also a few dinosaurs, including spinosaurs and other meat eaters. The bodies of many spinosaurs were suited to swimming, and their sharp teeth were perfect for feeding on fish.

The best-known reptiles from the Santana Formation are pterosaurs. Pterosaurs were flying reptiles, but guess what? They were *not* birds and they were *not* dinosaurs. They flew with wings formed by membranes that were attached to an elongate finger. Imagine if your ring finger was longer than you are tall! Pterosaur fossils are rare because their bones were hollow and had thin walls. However, many species have been found in the Santana Formation. Most of the Brazilian specimens had wingspans between 10 and 20 feet. Some, like *Anhanguera*, had thin, pointed teeth and probably caught fish. *Tapejara* had enormous vertical crests, which were mostly made of material like your fingernails. This unusual pterosaur is thought to have foraged for fruit and leaves.

DINO BREAKUP

When dinosaurs first appeared on Earth, all the continents were joined into the supercontinent Pangaea. This means that land animals were able to spread across the entire giant landmass. But during the Jurassic and Cretaceous, Pangaea split up, and by the end of the Cretaceous most of the continents were getting close to the positions they have on Earth today.

Separated by water, dinosaurs on the different continents began to evolve in different ways. In the Cretaceous, northern continents were dominated by tyrannosaurs, horned dinosaurs, duckbills, and armored dinosaurs. In southern continents, the meat-eating dinosaurs included sail-backed spinosaurs and short-armed abelisaurs, while the main herbivores were titanosaur sauropods, with a few armored and duck-billed dinosaurs.

IN FOCUS: PTEROSAURS

Besides dinosaurs, pterosaurs are the most famous of the extinct animals of the Mesozoic. Pterosaurs were covered in short fur-like fibers, and many had showy crests. They laid eggs, and at least some of them walked on all fours—using both their feet and their folded wings! The earliest pterosaurs had long tails, but later pterosaurs had practically no tails. People used to think that most pterosaurs were fish eaters, but we now know that they had many ways of life, like modern birds. Most of the known pterosaur fossils have been found in unusual rocks in Brazil, China, and Germany. For our terrarium, we will use a crested *Tapejara*. But there were many different types of pterosaurs and many of them come in toy versions. Do you recognize any of these?

- *Pteranodon* was one of the largest pterosaurs, with a wingspan greater than 20 feet. It's famous for its long, bony crest, and it patrolled the shallow continental sea in Late Cretaceous North America. Many toys include teeth in its jaws, but *Pteranodon* had no teeth. However, in the Brazilian rocks there's a pterosaur with a very similar crest as well as teeth, so these toys are accidentally accurate for another animal!

- *Pterodactylus* (the original "pterodactyl") is known from the Late Jurassic of Germany. It was a small pterosaur; its wingspan was only about 3 feet. It probably hunted small prey along the coast.

- *Quetzalcoatlus*, the largest known flying creature to live on Earth, had a wingspan of 30 to 35 feet and may have been the largest pterosaur. It had a long neck and skull, and it seems to have adapted to be a terrestrial hunter (something like a cross between a giraffe and a stork).

- *Rhamphorhynchus*, with a wingspan up to 6 feet, lived alongside *Pterodactylus* and is probably the best-known long-tailed pterosaur. It had a long skull with spiky, sharp teeth, and it caught fish.

Imagine fishing for Cretaceous fish along the Brazilian coast 100 million years ago. What sounds do you think the pterosaurs and spinosaurs made? Large and strange-looking pterosaurs would have flown overhead, and you would have had to keep an eye out for dinosaurs that wanted to steal your fish or chase you!

Many animals have lived along coastlines where the land meets the sea—both today and in the past. In these special places, land plants and animals live near the radically different environment of the ocean. This is why ancient coastal rocks can preserve both terrestrial and marine fossils.

Seaside Terrarium

Have you ever watched seabirds dive for fish or dolphins leap through the surf? Humans aren't the only ones who love the beach. Dinosaurs and pterosaurs hung out at the ocean too. A container, some sand, a few plants, and some shells are all you need to make a sandy seashore terrarium for a colorful flying *Tapejara*. If you don't have a *Tapejara*, feel free to substitute a *Pteranodon*, an *Anhanguera*, or a similar pterosaur. Let's head to the beach!

MATERIALS & TOOLS

1 container (glass, hard plastic, ceramic, or wood with a liner)

Pea gravel, aquarium gravel, or small pebbles

Cactus or succulent potting mix

1 to 3 small succulents

Washed aquarium sand
(white or tan for a "beach" look)

Blue glass beads, blue sand, or glittery blue gravel

Decorations of your choice:
shells, driftwood, coral, sand dollars,
chunky pebbles, sea glass, crystals, moss

Small branch and fishing wire (optional)

Toy pterosaur(s), miniature size

DIRECTIONS

1. If your container is made of glass, wash it well before starting. Line the bottom of your container with a ½-inch layer of pebbles or pea gravel. Pour a thin layer of cactus or succulent potting mix into the container.

2. Pop your plants out of their plastic liners and set them in the container. Before you plant, consider your design. When you're ready to commit, pour more succulent potting mix around the roots, pressing down gently with your fingers to remove any air pockets.

3. Pour a layer of sand carefully around your plants. Leave a little circle of uncovered soil around the base of each plant so that water can reach the roots.

4. Use your imagination to create your own unique seashore world for your pterosaur. Try using blue beads, sand, or gravel to make half your scene the ocean, and use white sand to make the other half a sandy shore. Add shells, coral, driftwood, and other beachy items.

5. To make your *Tapejara* fly, tie it to a branch with fishing wire so it dangles over the scene!

PLANT PICKS

Before you fill your shopping basket with miniature dune grasses, remember that grasses didn't yet exist during the middle part of the Cretaceous Period. Try starlike *Haworthia cymbiformis* or *Lithops,* a weird plant that looks like a pile of purple rocks. Dwarf aloe (*Aloe humilis*) and torch plant or lace aloe (*Aloe aristata*) look like wispy sea creatures, while fishhooks (*Senecio radicans*) resembles seaweed.

HAPPY SUCCULENTS

Did you know that succulents hate "wet feet"? This means they like soil that dries out quickly between waterings. Think about where succulents grow in the wild—dry, sandy places such as California and South Africa. To make your own succulent potting mix, get a bucket and stir together equal parts of regular potting soil, perlite, and crushed lava rock (or coarse sand, pumice, or poultry grit). Keep your succulent terrarium in bright indirect sunshine and water only when the soil is dry to the touch (about once a week or even less). Don't mist succulents. Misting and overwatering can lead to rot.

FUN IDEA

Tapejara and other pterosaurs made nests along the seashore. What about making a nest for your terrarium? What could you use to make eggs?

Colored Sand

Colored sand is easy to find at craft stores or online. But did you know you can use salt or white play sand to make an inexpensive version at home? You probably have all of these materials lying around the house. Reduce, reuse, and recycle—and have fun while you do it!

MATERIALS & TOOLS

Table salt or dry white sand

Large mason jars with lids, to shake the "sand"

Funnel

Food dye, tempera paint, colored school chalk, or chalk pastels

Containers to store your colored sand (the same mason jars used above, or smaller glass jars, clear storage containers, old yogurt tubs, or resealable plastic bags)

MAKE A FUNNEL

No funnel? No problem! You can make one with a piece of paper and some tape or a stapler. Curl a piece of paper into a long hot dog shape. Then gently squeeze and wiggle the roll until one end is wider and more open, while the other side comes together into a point with a small hole. Once the hole is the size you want, tape or staple your funnel into place.

DIRECTIONS

1. Using the funnel, pour some table salt or dry white sand into a large jar. Start with about 1 cup, depending on how much sand you plan to use for your project. Leave lots of space in the container for the salt or sand to move around when you shake it.

2. Add your dye (food dye, tempera paints, or chalk). If you want a darker color, add more dye. If you're using chalk and want a richer color, take a butter knife and carefully scrape some of the chalk into the salt.

3. Screw on the lid and shake, shake, shake! Put some music on and shake that jar until the sand is evenly tinted.

4. If you used paint, you'll need to let your colored sand dry. Spread it out on a cookie sheet or plate lined with a paper towel for a few hours or overnight until completely dry.

5. Store dry colored sand in containers. Now you have a rainbow just waiting for your project.

TIP: For younger children, the easiest method is to shake salt and food dye in a jar or plastic container with a lid. Just be careful not to let salt "sand" touch any plants you may use in your dino worlds.

DINO DOO-DOO

Everbody Poops, Even *Maiasaura*

AT A GLANCE

TIME	77 to 76 million years ago
PLACE	Montana
ROCKS	Two Medicine Formation
DINOSAURS	Carnivores (small): troodontids, dromaeosaurids Carnivores (large): *Daspletosaurus* Herbivores (small): *Orodromeus* Herbivores (large): *Maiasaura*
CO-STARRING	Woody plants Dung beetles Turtles Champsosaurs Early mammals
NOTABLE SITES	Egg Mountain

COMPOSTING IN
THE CRETACEOUS

If we took a time machine back to the Mesozoic we would see a variety of dinosaurs, many different plants, pterosaurs, insects, other animals, and guess what else? Dinosaur poop. Lots of dinosaur poop. Animals don't digest everything they eat, and undigested food has to be expelled. So all animals poop, and dinosaurs were no exception. Can poop be fossilized? Yes, under just the right conditions. Fossilized feces are called coprolites. But you don't have to turn up your nose because most fossil poop has been turned to rock, and it doesn't smell.

Coprolites from animals that lived on land are quite rare. The Cretaceous Two Medicine Formation of Montana is special because it preserved coprolites from herbivorous dinosaurs. It might seem funny to study ancient dung that's around 75 million years old, but coprolites can be gold mines of information about ancient ecosystems. The Two Medicine coprolites reveal that some plant-eating dinosaurs ate rotting wood. Distinctive burrows in the fossil feces also tell us that dung beetles helped recycle tons of dinosaur poop back into the ecosystem by burying and eating dung. Humans certainly don't eat poop, but it's good food for dung beetles. Who knows? Dung beetles might think that eating pizza is weird.

We usually can't tell what kinds of animals produced the poop that became coprolites. But our best guess is that duck-billed dinosaurs of the genus *Maiasaura* produced most of the ancient feces found in the Two Medicine Formation. *Maiasaura* could grow to 30 feet long, so they were large enough to produce poop masses that could be the size of a squished basketball. Those Two Medicine dung beetles had a lot to eat.

Other dinosaurs that lived with the *Maiasaura* included the small herbivore *Orodromeus* and the small carnivore *Troodon*. All the animals in the area would have had to keep an eye out for the scary tyrannosaur, *Daspletosaurus*, who hunted in the area. *Daspletosaurus* was smaller than *Tyrannosaurus rex* and lived in Montana and Canada 10 million years earlier than its famous cousin.

Studying the Two Medicine Formation coprolites reminds us that dinosaurs interacted with the plants and animals in their environment in different ways. The *Maiasaura* ate plants, and then their poop was eaten by dung beetles and snails. This helped recycle nutrients back into the ancient environment. This natural composting was just as important in the Cretaceous as it is today. Just imagine how much poop would build up if dung beetles and bacteria didn't convert dung into nutrients that fertilize plants!

WHO DUNG IT?

Paleontologist Dr. Karen Chin studies dinosaur coprolites. This is challenging because these fossils don't come with labels that tell us which type of animal produced the ancient poop. To figure out "who dung it," Dr. Chin has to analyze many clues, including coprolite size, what is preserved in the coprolite, and what other fossils are found in the area.

THE "GOOD MOTHER" DINOSAUR

Maiasaura means "good mother lizard" or "caring mother lizard." This name was chosen because fossil evidence shows that these dinosaurs stayed in their nesting grounds to care for their babies. The baby *Maiasaura* would have needed protection because they were only about 1½ feet long when they hatched from their eggs.

CAN YOU GUESS?

Question: Can paleontologists tell what kind of dinosaur laid a particular egg?
Answer: It isn't always easy to tell what kind of dinosaur laid an egg. One kind of egg from the Two Medicine Formation was first thought to have come from *Orodromeus*, but it later turned out that they were *Troodon* eggs instead.

WOOD FOR DINNER? YUCK

Some coprolites probably left by *Maiasaura* contain lots of wood. Wood normally is hard to eat, but this wood was "predigested" by a fungus that rotted it, making it more nutritious. Rotten wood for dinner might sound pretty gross to you, but the *Maiasaura* loved it.

Forest Floor Terrarium

Imagine you're walking through a quiet forest. Tall trees surround you on all sides. Look up and feel warm sunlight filtering down through a canopy of leaves. Now stoop down and look carefully at the forest floor. Notice how the ground feels soft and spongy under your feet. That's because it's covered with rotting leaves and new sprouts. The forest is constantly breaking down things that have died or decayed and turning them into nutrients for new life. Forests are also full of animals. Those animals poop every day. As you build a thick forest terrarium for your "good mother lizard," the *Maiasaura*, don't forget to include homemade coprolites (dino poop). Watch your step!

MATERIALS & TOOLS

1 container (glass, hard plastic, ceramic, or wood with a liner)

Pea gravel, aquarium gravel, or small pebbles

Potting soil

3 to 5 miniature evergreen plants

Decorations of your choice: sticks or small branches, tiny pebbles for eggs, pine cones, rocks, moss, blue glass beads, feathers, leaves

Coprolites (Dino Poop)
(see page 61 for activity)

Toy dinosaur(s), miniature size (plus a regular size for the "mother," optional)

TIP: This forest terrarium needs abundant sunshine. Aim to water about once a week, when the soil is dry to the touch. Watch carefully, and in a few months you'll notice your miniature forest has grown taller.

DIRECTIONS

1. If possible, wash your container with soap and hot water before starting. If you can't wash it, then wipe it clean with a rag. Cover the bottom of the container with a ½-inch layer of pebbles or gravel and a thin layer of potting soil.

2. Pop your plants out of their plastic liners and arrange them in the container. Pour soil around the roots, pushing down gently with your fingers to hold the plants in place. Add more soil until the soil level reaches the base of the plants.

3. There's more to a forest than trees. What about some fallen logs, a stream or pond made out of blue glass beads, or a cave shaped from rocks and moss? Look around your terrarium. If you were a *Maiasaura*, where would you build the safest, coziest nest? What materials would you use? Have fun building a cozy nest with feathers, moss, or leaves. And don't forget the coprolites!

4. Set your dinosaur toys into the habitat you've created and act out a scene. If you'd like to include a *Maiasaura* mother and baby, include both a regular-sized dinosaur toy and a miniature one.

PLANT PICKS

The earliest known conifers appeared around 300 million years ago, before the Triassic Period began. Conifers are gymnosperms, which means they have cones. Conifer trees still live today. While the earliest conifers looked different from modern ones, they were the ancestors of the pine, spruce, fir, and other evergreen trees you see in the forest today.

Check out the terrarium or bonsai section of a well-stocked nursery and you'll find lots of wonderful plants that look like tiny conifer trees. Compact fernspray cypress (*Chamaecyparis obtusa* 'Filicoides Compacta'), miniature common spruce (*Juniperus communis* 'Miniature'), and dwarf Atlantic white cedar (*Chamaecyparis thyoides* 'Top Point') are all fun choices. (See "Modern Plant Look-Alikes," page xxi, for more options.) Miniature lemon cypress (*Cupressus macrocarpa* 'Goldcrest') is special. Rub the leaves gently between your fingers and you'll breathe in a delicious lemon scent.

Coprolites (Dino Poop)

Everybody poops. Even dinosaurs. And what happened to dino poop? Most of it was recycled back into the environment, but if the conditions were right, some of it turned to rock. A poop fossil is called a coprolite. Can you imagine if your poop was discovered millions of years from now and studied under microscopes? Well, that's what happens to dinosaur poop. You can learn a lot about a dinosaur by studying what you find in its poop.

So, what are you waiting for? It's time to make some coprolites!

MATERIALS & TOOLS

1 cup flour

1 cup salt

⅔ cup cornstarch

⅔ cup warm water

Decorations of your choice: toy beetles, dried rice, twigs, nuts, grass, dried noodles

Poop-colored acrylic paint and paintbrush (optional)

Rolling pin (optional)

STOP! SAVE THE DOUGH

Don't toss that extra salt dough! You can use salt dough to make trees, ornaments, objects, or sculptures. See "Baked Tracks," page 19, to make tracks and "Salt Dough Ammonite," page 29, to make an ammonite. Store extra salt dough in an airtight container or resealable plastic bag.

DIRECTIONS

1. Stir together the flour, salt, cornstarch, and water in a large bowl. If the dough feels too crumbly, add a little more water. If it's too sticky, add a little more flour.

2. Divide into individual hunks of dough and knead until smooth and elastic. Use a rolling pin or your hands to form the dough into poop shapes.

3. Add "texture." Ever see corn in your poop after you've eaten corn on the cob? It's the same with dinosaurs. Not everything gets digested. Get creative with your decorations to make your coprolites look like real poop.

4. Let the dough harden. There are two ways you can do this. Preheat the oven to 250°F and bake your coprolites on a lightly greased or parchment-lined baking sheet for 20 to 40 minutes, until hard and dry. (Younger children, please ask an adult to help you.) Or set out your coprolites (uncovered) and let them dry naturally for a few days. Be sure to flip them over to dry both sides completely.

5. Once your coprolites are hard as rocks, pull out your paints and paintbrush, if desired, and see how realistic you can make the poop look. Then find them a good spot in your forest terrarium.

CRETACEOUS CLASH

Tyrannosaurus Rex and Triceratops Fight to the Death

AT A GLANCE

TIME	68 to 66 million years ago
PLACE	Western United States (Montana, South Dakota, Wyoming)
ROCKS	Hell Creek Formation Lance Formation
DINOSAURS	Carnivores (small): dromaeosaurs, ostrich-mimics Carnivores (medium): *Anzu, Dakotaraptor* Carnivores (large): *Tyrannosaurus* Herbivores (small): *Leptoceratops, Pachycephalosaurus, Thescelosaurus* Herbivores (large): *Ankylosaurus, Edmontosaurus, Torosaurus, Triceratops*
CO-STARRING	Ferns, conifers, and flowering plants Turtles Champsosaurs Crocodilians Pterosaurs Small mammals
NOTABLE SITES	Makoshika State Park

VIOLENT CHANGE

Tyrannosaurus rex and *Triceratops* roamed the earth at the very end of the Cretaceous. At this time, the seaway that used to divide western and eastern North America was drying up and mountain-building forces were causing the rise of the Rocky Mountains. Between the growing mountains and the shrinking sea, rivers flowed across broad areas of flat land. Forests of broadleaf flowering trees flourished, with abundant ferns in the undergrowth. The dinosaurs living in these warm, lush forests didn't know it, but they were the last dinosaurs before the great extinction.

Three dinosaurs were especially abundant in North America during the last part of the Cretaceous: *Tyrannosaurus*, *Triceratops*, and the large crestless duck-billed *Edmontosaurus*. Several other kinds of dinosaurs are also known from good fossils. They include the armored and club-tailed *Ankylosaurus*; *Anzu*, a birdlike theropod dinosaur larger than an ostrich, with a helmetlike crest; the small hornless "horned dinasaur" *Leptoceratops*; the bonehead *Pachycephalosaurus*; the small but sturdy beaked herbivore *Thescelosaurus*; and *Torosaurus*, a large horned dinosaur very similar to *Triceratops*. There are also scrappy fossils of small predatory dinosaurs, but they are difficult to identify.

Crocodilians, turtles, monitor lizards, and champsosaurs (something like a cross between a large lizard and a gharial, a long-snouted crocodilian) lived with these dinosaurs. Giant pterosaurs with wingspans up to 30 feet were equally at home on the ground and in the air, where diverse birds also could be found. Mammals were still opossum-sized or smaller.

Everyone assumes that the *Tyrannosaurus* and *Triceratops* fought each other. But how do we know this? There's a *Triceratops* specimen with tooth marks on the frill and partially healed damage to a brow horn, so it must have survived for at least a while after the fight.

How did these huge creatures battle each other? Fully grown *Tyrannosaurus* and *Triceratops* were enormous animals, each weighing several tons. At these sizes, speed was probably limited to short bursts. It takes a lot of energy to get that kind of bulk moving quickly, and falling or stumbling could have easily broken bones. A large *Tyrannosaurus* may have tried to ambush a *Triceratops* at close range, instead of charging through the open and letting the *Triceratops* prepare for the attack. The predator probably preferred to attack from the rear or sides, to make a devastating strike and then get away, or even to knock over the horned dinosaur.

On the defensive side, *Triceratops* was a plant eater, but it was no bunny rabbit. This large herbivore was probably more maneuverable than *Tyrannosaurus* because it had a lower center of gravity and walked on four legs. We can imagine it pivoting to keep its horns and powerful beak facing an attacking *Tyrannosaurus*, tossing its head like a buffalo or bull while the tyrannosaur looked for an opening or planned a retreat. An encounter between partially grown *Tyrannosaurus* and *Triceratops* could have been much more athletic, although the basic strategies were probably similar: a surprise first strike for the *Tyrannosaurus*, a headfirst defense for the *Triceratops*.

BISON OR DINOSAUR?

Othniel Charles Marsh described the first fossils of *Triceratops*, a pair of horns. He thought the rocks they came from were young, and he reported the fossils as enormous bison horns. Wrong.

FLOWER POWER

When you think of plants, you probably think of ones that have flowers. But flowering plants were actually late additions to life on Earth. Although there are hints that flowering plants appeared in the Triassic or Jurassic, the oldest fossils we definitely know came from flowering plants date to the Early Cretaceous, around 130 million years ago. Flowering plants spread quickly, and by the end of the Late Cretaceous, they were diverse and abundant enough to be major forest plants. The key features of flowering plants are their flowers and fruits. Many flowering plants can attract insects and other animals with their sweet nectar or tasty fruits. Animals then unknowingly do the plants a favor by spreading pollen or seeds. It is amazing how plants have managed to make animals work for them!

CAN YOU GUESS?

Question: Which dinosaur bone is the most commonly found?
Answer: *Triceratops* skull parts are some of the most common dinosaur fossils. However, the rest of the skeleton is much rarer—all skeletons on display in museums are combinations of multiple skeletons!

BONE CRUSHER

Most theropod teeth were thin, but *Tyrannosaurus* teeth were like thick steak knives. These special teeth—plus its strong skull—allowed it to crush bones. We can see evidence of this behavior in one of the biggest dinosaur coprolites, which is full of bone fragments.

LOST AND FOUND

It can take decades or more to go through all the fossils from an expedition. In 1891, paleontologists uncovered and crated up a small dinosaur skeleton from the Late Cretaceous of Wyoming. The crate wasn't opened until about 20 years later, and the scientist who rediscovered it named it *Thescelosaurus neglectus,* the "neglected marvelous lizard."

PLANT PORTRAIT:
Amborella Trichopoda

Amborella trichopoda is a species of flowering plant found only on Grande-Terre, one of the islands of New Caledonia in the southwest Pacific. It is a shrub or tree that has long narrow leaves and small white flowers. *Amborella trichopoda* is special because it seems to be the flowering plant most like the earliest flowering plants that appeared millions of years ago in the Mesozoic.

Cliffside Battle Terrarium

Imagine a warm jungle woodland full of lush flowers and buzzing insects. Have you ever visited the coast of Louisiana or other southern states? That's probably similar to how our Cretaceous forest would have looked. In this project, you'll build a cliffside Cretaceous hideaway for the three-horned giant, the *Triceratops*. But watch out! The mighty *Tyrannosaurus rex* lurks behind a boulder, ready to attack. The plant-eating *Triceratops* and massive *T. rex* were fierce enemies. These dinosaurs roamed over woodland terrain during the Late Cretaceous. Remember that before the Cretaceous Period, there were few—if any—flowers on Earth. Have fun picking out flowering plants for your dino world. Then set up a cliffside battle scene for your hungry *T. rex* and the big-headed *Triceratops*.

TOY TALK

TOP TOYS: *Tyrannosaurus rex* and *Triceratops*
SUBSTITUTES: *Tyrannosaurus rex* and *Triceratops*, corpse edition

TIP: Before watering or misting your plants, brush any dirt off the glass or the leaves of the plants. You can buy stylish terrarium tools at specialty garden centers, but a dry, thick, soft paintbrush works just as well.

TRUE OR FALSE?

If it's not in a closed container, it's not a terrarium.
Answer: True (technically). Gregg "Roosevelt" Harris, the owner of Roosevelt's Terrariums in Portland, Oregon, says, "If it doesn't have a lid, who you trying to kid? It's not a terrarium." A Wardian case is one type of terrarium. Corked glass jugs or apothecary jars are also terrariums. British gardener David Latimer hasn't watered his thriving bottle terrarium since 1972! Technically, open containers are called dish gardens. However, many people use the term *terrarium* to refer to any miniature garden or dish garden, sealed or not.

MATERIALS & TOOLS

1 Wardian case, glass terrarium house, or clear container with high sides and a lid

Pea gravel, aquarium gravel, or small pebbles

Activated charcoal

Perlite

Potting soil

1 to 3 large rocks, plus some medium-sized stones, to make a cliff

1 to 3 miniature plants with flowers

1 or 2 live moss plants, such as delicate fern or pincushion moss (optional)

Decorations of your choice: decorative gravel, rocks, preserved moss, sand, minerals, gems, coprolites (page 61), tiny pebbles, sticks, seedlings, pine cones

Blue stones, blue clay, blue Salt Dough (see page 19 for recipe), or blue slime (see "Stuck in the Slime," page 80, for recipe), to make a water feature (optional)

Toy dinosaurs, miniature size

PLANT PICKS

Tropical plants are perfect for this dino world. Have you ever seen a sensitive plant (*Mimosa pudica*)? If you haven't, you must find one. Touch the leaves and they curl in on themselves! A tiny African violet (*Saintpaulia ionantha*), miniature calla lily (*Zantedeschia aethiopica*), or miniature orchid (there are many varieties) adds drama and elegance. Try a purple or green miniature shamrock (*Oxalis regnellii*). This lucky plant resembles a tiny ginkgo, but with the added benefit that it blooms with tiny white flowers (remember,

the Late Cretaceous is all about flowers). Don't forget all the Triassic and Jurassic look-alikes such as ferns, mosses, horsetail, and cycads (see "Modern Plant Look-Alikes," page xxi), as those were still around during the Cretaceous Period. Miniature tropicals are found in the terrarium or fairy garden section of your local garden center. You can find larger specimens at big-box garden centers too. Just make sure your chosen plants share similar light and moisture needs.

DIRECTIONS

1. Wash your container with soap and hot water until it is sparkling clean. Allow to dry. Pour a 1-inch layer of gravel into the container. Top the gravel with a sprinkle of activated charcoal, followed by a band of perlite to keep the layers distinct. Finish with a layer of potting soil. (See "Layer Cake Method," page xxii, for more details.)

2. Use larger rocks and medium stones to create a cliff or small mountain terrace. Keep checking out the layers from the side to make sure you like how it looks. Whether you're aiming for a jagged cliff or small terrace, it's a good idea to use larger stones to build a firm foundation. Pea gravel will slip but rocks or chunky pebbles will hold firm. Keep in mind that once you add water to your terrarium, gravity will pull everything down. So if you want a hill or canyon, make your foundation layer steeper than you think you should.

3. Pop your plants out of their plastic liners and play around until you find the right arrangement. Dig holes in the soil layer and tuck in the plants. Sprinkle more soil around the roots, pushing down gently with your fingers to hold the plants in place. Add more soil until it reaches the base of the plants. If desired, place live moss on top of the soil layer, pressing gently. Add another layer of decorative gravel or tiny stones, if desired.

4. What kind of background would look exciting for your cliffside battle? A cave or den? Some plants to hide behind? A fallen log to escape an attack? A gushing waterfall or pool? A crystal or sparkly gem? Once your background is arranged, set your dinosaurs up for battle.

WARDIAN CASE

Do you know the story behind enclosed terrariums? In the 1830s, Dr. Nathaniel Ward, an English surgeon, used glass jars to hold the moths he liked to collect. This was the era of scientific discovery when anyone could be a naturalist. All sorts of regular people were traipsing across the countryside—and the world—collecting fossils, butterflies, and flowers. Don't let anyone tell you that you can't be a naturalist, too. Start today!

One day, Dr. Ward stumbled upon an old case he had forgotten about. Inside, unwatered for months, a fern had survived! Dr. Ward had accidentally discovered the basic principle of enclosed terrariums: Plants create water as a by-product of photosynthesis. That moisture evaporates. With no place to escape, it turns into condensation, which cools, runs down the glass, and dribbles back into the soil. This world under glass is self-sustaining and self-watering.

Dr. Ward published his findings, and soon botanists were using Wardian cases to transport rare orchids and other plants from the tropics. Victorians were bewitched by the beauty of terrariums, Wardian cases, and ferneries. They used them for both science and home decoration.

Have you ever read Jan Brett's picture book *Mossy*? It's packed with intricate illustrations of classic Wardian cases. They became a coveted design trend, and now, nearly 200 years later, they're back in style.

Leaf Hunt and Gratitude Tree

Fall means cozy sweaters, hot cider, pumpkins, and apple picking. This is a perfect activity to do around Thanksgiving, when autumn leaves are glowing red and gold, but it's equally fun any time of year. Next time you're outside in your neighborhood or at a park, go on a leaf hunt. Slow down, look around, and notice how many different leaf shapes you can observe and collect. Then use your treasures to create a gratitude tree. Pause for a few moments each day. Reflect on something you're grateful for. Write it down on a paper leaf and add it to your tree. Gratitude is contagious! The more we stop to notice all the blessings in our lives, the more joy and contentment we will feel.

MATERIALS & TOOLS

"Tree" of your choice

Leaves

Colored card stock or construction paper

Pencil

Scissors

Hole punch, string, or tape (optional)

DIRECTIONS

1. Start by finding or making the trunk and branches of your tree. Stroll around your house, yard, or neighborhood. Use your imagination. Is there anything lying around that you could turn into a tree trunk? What about a beautiful branch or a fragrant rosemary plant, potted in a pretty container? My husband made our tree out of a rock and some wire. We set it out every November and add paper leaves all month long. For a simpler version, trace the outline of a trunk and branches on a large piece of paper and tape it to the wall or a window. Get creative to find or make a tree that's unique to your family.

2. Now it's time to add leaves to your tree trunk and branches. Go on a leaf hunt! Grab a basket and see how many different shapes, colors, and sizes you can collect. You'll be surprised when you stop to notice the incredible variety of leaves you can find. Bring home your leaves.

3. Before they have a chance to shrivel up, set your leaves on colored card stock. Use a pencil to trace them, then use scissors to cut out paper leaves. (A simple leaf shape makes for a much faster process!)

4. Set a pile of paper leaves and a pen next to your gratitude tree. Every morning, or after dinner, or just anytime you feel like it, write down something you're grateful for and add it to the tree. (Punch holes in the leaves to hang them on wire or real tree; use tape to attach to a paper one.) Friends and guests will want to add their notes too. Within a few weeks, your tree will be glowing with leaves.

TIP: Leaves with simple shapes (such as the aspen leaves we find in Colorado) will be easier to trace and cut.

FLOWERING TREES

Nearly all of the beautiful deciduous leaves we notice in the fall come from broad-leaved flowering trees. Flowering plants can be as small as a dandelion or as giant as an oak tree. The term *deciduous* comes from the Latin word for "fall off" and every autumn, that's what happens: these majestic trees drop their leaves. Remember, flowering plants did not spread across the earth until the Cretaceous Period. Maybe your first paper leaf should express gratitude that flowering trees evolved!

....

AFTER YOU TRACE THE TREE LEAVES . . . PRESERVE THEM!

Press real tree leaves between sheets of paper. Set them carefully inside a heavy book such as an encyclopedia or cookbook. Set more heavy books on top and let them rest for a few days. Use the preserved leaves for decoration around the house. Or tuck them inside a card with a quick note telling someone what you appreciate about them. Mail it off with a smile. You've brightened someone's day!

DINO MUMMIES AND WORMY CARCASSES

What Happens When a *Brachylophosaurus* Dies?

AT A GLANCE

TIME	78 to 76 million years ago
PLACE	Montana
ROCKS	Judith River Formation
DINOSAURS	Carnivores (small): troodontids Carnivores (large): tyrannosaurs Herbivores (large): *Brachylophosaurus, Judiceratops, Medusaceratops, Zuul*
CO-STARRING	Conifers and flowering plants Guitarfish Garfish Turtles Champsosaurs Crocodilians
NOTABLE SITES	Malta

FROM LIVING CREATURE
TO FOSSIL

You've probably seen dinosaur fossils in a museum or on TV. But how do we get from a dead dinosaur carcass to a fossil? What happens when a dinosaur dies?

For a dinosaur or any other living thing to become a fossil, some part of it must be preserved in sediment. This can happen in many ways: in ooze at the seafloor, in sediment in a river, in sand dunes, and sometimes even in layers of volcanic ash. Quick burial is the key, because it helps protect tissues from scavenging or rapid decay. It also helps if the organism had some kind of sturdy body part, such as a shell, bones, or wood. For example, animals such as clams and snails have a much better chance of becoming fossils than jellyfish, which have no hard parts. Dinosaur lovers are happy that dinosaurs had tough, fossilizable bones.

In some ways, any fossil of a large land animal is unusual. Think of all the nonavian dinosaurs that must have lived during the 170 million years or so between their appearance and the extinction at the end of the Cretaceous. The number of dinosaur fossils that are in museums or are still in the ground is just a tiny fraction of this. There were many types of dinosaurs we will never know about because they lived in the wrong environments for fossilization, or because the rocks that contained their fossils have eroded. As we saw in chapter 2, some dinosaurs are only known from their footprints. Many others are only known from teeth. Because most dinosaurs had teeth that continuously replaced, they would leave behind many more shed teeth in a lifetime than bones. (Of course, toothless dinosaurs don't count!)

Many dinosaurs are only known from a handful of bones or teeth. This is because dinosaur carcasses were usually pulled apart by scavengers and then decayed, leaving only a few pieces that could be preserved. Sometimes insects bored into bones and destroyed them. Under rare lucky conditions, a carcass was buried by sediment so the nearly complete skeleton was preserved in a life-like position. Even more rarely, sometimes impressions of soft tissues such as skin became preserved. These impressions may be more common than we think, though, because in the past, people who wanted to study the fossils often cleaned off all the rock and sediment from skeletons, leaving just bones.

The rarest of all dinosaur fossils are "mummies." They're called mummies because they resemble natural human mummies, which form in protected dry environments. Dinosaur mummies are covered with impressions of soft tissues, allowing us to see the shapes of muscles and other body structures, and skin patterns. For reasons we can't explain, most of the handful of mummified dinosaurs are duck-billed or armored dinosaurs. None of the mummies are complete, which isn't surprising when you think about how big these animals were in life, and some of the soft tissue impressions have been removed by preparation for display and study. Some of the mummies have what look like the remains of the dinosaur's last meal inside them, although this can be difficult to prove because carcasses usually open up as they decompose, allowing things to go in or out.

> ## TRUE OR FALSE?
> Without sediment, there could be no dinosaur fossil.
> Answer: True. Sediment can be dirt, ash, rock, mud, silt, gravel, or sand—any kind of material that settles to the bottom of a liquid. In order to become a fossil, some part of a dinosaur must be preserved in sediment.

FIRST BUT STILL MYSTERIOUS

The Judith River Formation was one of the first dinosaur-producing rock units to be explored in the United States, but many of its dinosaurs are poorly known. They look similar to slightly younger dinosaurs from Alberta, Canada.

BOTTOM OF THE SEA

Fossils have sometimes been destroyed in wars, usually when the museum holding them is damaged or destroyed. In 1916, during World War I, the SS *Mount Temple* was bound for England with a cargo that included possible duck-billed dinosaur mummies. Unfortunately, it was sunk by a German submarine, and the fossils are still at the bottom of the Atlantic.

BRAND-NEW DINOSAUR!
BOREALOPELTA

As we were writing this book, a mummy of a new kind of armored dinosaur was described. This dinosaur, named *Borealopelta*, was discovered by accident in northeastern Alberta, Canada, during mining activity! It lived about 100 million years ago and was about 18 feet long. Its carcass was washed into a sea, where it sank and settled on its back. This dinosaur was covered in bony scutes, spikes, and platelike pieces of armor, including a long spike over each shoulder. The exact layout of its armor is preserved. Chemical traces in the specimen suggest that *Borealopelta* was reddish on top and lighter colored below, a kind of camouflage called countershading. Countershading is found today in many smaller animals, so if this dinosaur was countershaded, it probably means it was in danger of attack, even though it was heavily armored.

IN FOCUS: LEONARDO THE *BRACHYLOPHOSAURUS* MUMMY

Paleontologist Justin Tweet studied "Leonardo," a mummy of a *Brachylophosaurus* duck-billed dinosaur that had a broad flat crest on its head. Leonardo was found in the Judith River Formation of Montana and lived around 77 million years ago. The Judith River Formation records a warm, humid time in a land with many rivers. The Western Interior Seaway wasn't too far away to the east, and conifers such as cypresses mixed with flowering plants in the swampy lowlands. Volcanoes to the west sometimes filled the landscape with ash. Living at about the same time as Leonardo were freshwater guitarfish (*Myledaphus*), bony fish (including a gar that was found in another *Brachylophosaurus* skeleton, probably from getting trapped in the carcass while scavenging), salamanders, turtles, lizards, the gavial-like aquatic reptile *Champsosaurus*, crocodilians, and several kinds of dinosaurs, including tyrannosaurs, small theropods, horned dinosaurs, and armored dinosaurs.

Leonardo's body cavity was found to be full of fingernail-sized plant fragments. The fragments were poorly preserved, but they appear to be mostly pieces of leaves. One scientist suggested in the 1960s that duck-billed dinosaurs could feed by clamping their beaks over branches, pulling back, and stripping off leaves before grinding them up with their teeth. Feeding like this could produce something like what we see in Leonardo. The material inside Leonardo also included hundreds of tiny burrows about a third of a millimeter across. These were made by tiny wormy animals, and it seems likely that the worms were parasites that were moving around in the carcass. Yuck!

River Run Terrarium

Let's create a river scene for a flat-headed herbivore such as *Brachylophosaurus* or an armored dinosaur such as *Borealopelta*. Your unlucky *Brachylophosaurus* might get stuck in gooey sediment or washed downstream after an epic battle. Maybe it will even turn into a mummy like Leonardo. Before you get started, decide if you want to create a plunging waterfall, a trickling stream, or a lazy riverbank. You'll need to use rocks to build a strong foundation before adding soil and blue pebbles to your dino world. Once you've created your river, add mud, trees, plants, islands, fallen logs, quicksand—whatever your imagination can dream up!

TOY TALK

NOTE: Tiny toys of *Brachylophosaurus* or *Borealopelta* are hard to get, but almost all generic tubes or tubs of miniature toy dinosaurs contain at least 1 flat-headed herbivore or an armored dinosaur.
TOP TOY: A flat-headed herbivore such as *Edmontosaurus* or *Iguanodon*
SUBSTITUTES: An armored dinosaur (ankylosaur) such as *Ankylosaurus* or *Polacanthus*

MATERIALS & TOOLS

1 clear container (glass or clear hard plastic with high sides)

Pea gravel, aquarium gravel, or clean pebbles

Activated charcoal

Perlite

Potting soil

Large rocks for foundation

Blue modeling clay, blue Salt Dough (see page 19 for activity), or blue slime for the riverbed (see "Stuck in the Slime," page 80, for activity)

Pebbles (white, blue, or green), crystals, or blue glitter

3 to 5 miniature plants

Brown or black slime for mud or sediment trap (see "Stuck in the Slime," page 80, for activity) (optional)

Decorations of your choice: decorative sand, tiny glittery pebbles, sticks, seedlings, pine cones, rocks, leaves

Toy dinosaur(s), miniature size

DIRECTIONS

1. Wash your container with soap and hot water until it's sparkling clean. Dry with a clean towel. Pour a 1-inch layer of gravel into the container. Top the gravel with a sprinkle of activated charcoal, followed by a band of perlite to keep the layers distinct. Finish with a layer of potting soil. Make additional layers now, if you like that look, but be sure to finish with a soil layer. (See "Layer Cake Method," page xxii, for more details.)

2. Before adding your plants, make an elevated riverbed. Use larger rocks and gravel to stack one side of the terrarium higher than the other, so that your river will have a path to run down. If you'd like to make a waterfall, use larger rocks to build the foundation now. Blue salt dough or blue slime makes a fantastic riverbed. Press blue dough or slime into a riverbed shape and lay it over the cliffs to make a waterfall, pond, or river. Sprinkle the riverbed with white, blue, or green pebbles, crystals, or glitter (or a combination!) to add sparkle.

3. Pop your plants out of their plastic liners and play around until you find the right arrangement. Dig holes in the soil layer and tuck in the plants. Sprinkle more soil around the roots, pushing down gently with your fingers to hold the plants in place. Add more soil until it reaches the base of the plants.

4. What about making an island for your dinosaur to hide from predators, a patch of quicksand, or a gooey slime trap? What if your dinosaur got stuck in a bog or mud pit? You could even pour real water down your riverbed and see if your dinosaur gets trapped in the sediment. Let your toy dinosaurs loose in the terrarium and see what happens.

PLANT PICKS

Since we're now in the flourishing Cretaceous Period, you can go crazy with lots of plant varieties. (For a detailed list of suggestions, see "Modern Look-Alikes," page xxi.) Just remember to include a stream or pond in your design, since the Judith River Formation had many rivers. If you add a mud trap or slimy sediment (see page 8 for activity), be sure to keep it from touching (and harming) your plants.

MAKE YOUR OWN DINO MUMMY

To make a Halloween-type dinosaur mummy, cut out thin strips of plain muslin fabric or white paper, or grab white ribbon or string. Use glue or tape to attach one end of the fabric, paper, or ribbon to your dinosaur, then carefully wind the strips all the way around until it looks like a mummy. Tuck in the end or secure with more glue. Just remember that real dinosaur "mummies" looked like dried carcasses. They didn't have bandages! (For more ideas on how to customize your dinosaur toys, see "Designer Dinos," page 40.)

NICKNAMES

Well-preserved dinosaur skeletons sometimes get nicknames. Leonardo's nickname comes from nearby graffiti left by "Leonard Webb" over a hundred years ago.

Stuck in the Slime

Have you ever heard of the La Brea Tar Pits in Los Angeles? Over I million bones have been pulled from the pits, including bones from saber-toothed cats. The La Brea bones are much, much younger than dinosaur fossils—only 50,000 to 11,000 years old. But that's still really old in human years!

No dinosaur fossils have been found in tar pits. But the world's highest concentration of Jurassic fossils was found in the Cleveland-Lloyd Dinosaur Quarry of Utah. Many scientists believe those unlucky dinosaurs got stuck in a giant prehistoric mud hole. Wouldn't it be cool to add some quicksand, mud quarries, or sticky sink holes to your dino world? Let's make homemade slime so you can dream up some gooey traps.

You'll love how squidgy and cool this feels in your hands. This recipe makes a full batch, so think of all the other fun ways you can play with this goo. Tint it blue and you can use it to shape a riverbed for your terrarium. Dye it black and you're looking at a mud trap. Experiment with clear glue versus opaque. Try cutting it with scissors or cookie cutters, coloring it with markers, or adding glitter. Another fun way to use the slime is to lay it out in a slab and blow bubbles into it with a large straw. How big can you make your bubble before it pops?

MATERIALS & TOOLS

½ cup nontoxic school glue (clear or opaque)

½ cup warm water

Liquid watercolor or food dye

½ teaspoon baking soda

1 scant tablespoon contact lens solution (must contain boric acid or sodium borate)

Large straws (optional)

DIRECTIONS

1. Empty the glue container into a large mixing bowl. Stir in the warm water and a few drops of food dye. If you want to add glitter, now is the time.

2. Add the baking soda and mix well, then add the contact solution just a tiny bit at a time. Stir vigorously. It will start to come together into a solid mass. You might be tempted to squeeze in more contact lens solution. Don't. Stir instead. Once it starts pulling away from the sides of the bowl, knead it until it feels like slime.

3. Stretch it! Bounce it! Roll it!

4. Store slime in a large resealable plastic bag or airtight container.

END OF THE WORLD
After All The Titanosaurs Died

AT A GLANCE

TIME	66 million years ago
PLACE	Western and central India
ROCKS	Lameta Formation
DINOSAURS	Carnivores (small): *Laevisuchus* Carnivores (large): *Rahiolisaurus, Rajasaurus* Herbivores (large): *Isisaurus, Jainosaurus,* unnamed egg-layers
CO-STARRING	Early grasses Turtles Large constricting snakes (*Madtsoia, Sanajeh*)
NOTABLE SITES	Deccan Plateau, India

TOTAL EXTINCTION

The dinosaur world of the Mesozoic came to a catastrophic end 66 million years ago. It's hard to believe that the majestic, nonavian dinosaurs all went extinct at that time, but did you know that they weren't the only victims? Pterosaurs, plesiosaurs, mosasaurs, ammonites, and many other animals and plants also went extinct at the same time.

The cause of this great extinction has been debated for a long time. People have proposed almost everything from A (alien hunters) to Z (zapped by cosmic rays)! But geologic evidence suggests two major reasons for the extinction. The most important was that an asteroid about 6 miles in diameter hit Earth 66 million years ago, wreaking havoc on Earth's environment. In addition, huge volcanic eruptions in India also pumped out harmful gases that damaged Earth's climate. The terrible conditions on Earth at the end of the Cretaceous caused more than 60 percent of all species on Earth to die out.

You already know from chapter 7 that *Tyrannosaurus* and *Triceratops* lived in North America at the very end of the Cretaceous. On the other side of Earth, a large piece of land that had broken from Africa was slowly moving north. Today we would recognize that mass of land as India and parts of its neighbors. At the same time that *Tyrannosaurus* hunted in Montana, huge amounts of lava flowed from volcanic vents across much of India. As much as half of India was covered in volcanic rocks. Fossils from the Lameta Formation show that some of India's dinosaurs lived near this volcanic activity.

Because India had been separated from other landmasses for millions of years, it had its own unique dinosaurs. No beaked dinosaurs (such as duck-billed or horned dinosaurs) are known for certain. Instead, there were many kinds of carnivorous theropods and herbivorous sauropods. The carnivores were all abelisaurs, a group mostly limited to the southern continents. Some of them were human-sized or smaller, but we know very little about them. Larger abelisaurs were more like *Allosaurus* in size. They often had short, tall skulls, and their arms were tiny like tyrannosaur arms. Some abelisaurs had horns or knobs on their heads.

The herbivores from the Lameta Formation were titanosaurs. We know that these sauropods—including some of the smallest and the largest we know of—were wider and tubbier than the ones in North America. *Isisaurus* is one of the better-known titanosaurs. Unlike most sauropods, *Isisaurus* seems to have been built something like a ramp, angled down from the head and neck to the hips and tail. Fossilized eggs of Indian sauropods have also been found.

It's sad that the many intriguing and often gigantic dinosaurs of the Mesozoic went extinct. Most of us would love to see what those dinosaurs looked like in the flesh. But we can look out our windows today and see a variety of birds hopping and flying around. These birds are the dinosaurs that survived the mass extinction at the end of the Cretaceous.

GRASS

Did you know that grasses are flowering plants? Although grasses are common today, they didn't appear until late in the Cretaceous. We know they were growing in India then because we have found traces of grass in fossilized feces from the Lameta Formation.

ARMS WITH NO WRIST?

That's right. Abelisaur arms were almost all upper arm. Their forearms, hands, and fingers were shrunken, and they had no wrist bones! What could you do with an arm like that?

NESTING SAUROPODS

Titanosaur eggs and nests have been discovered in the Lameta Formation of India. Nesting grounds attracted other animals. A partial skeleton of a large fossil snake has been found near a nest and hatchling titanosaur, and a crocodile nest has been found among titanosaur nests.

Erupting Volcano Terrarium

Most paleontologists agree that the main cause of dinosaur extinction was the giant asteroid that hit Mexico. But erupting volcanos in what is now India certainly didn't help matters. Get ready for a river of molten red lava! For this terrarium, we will build a dino world complete with a volcano that actually erupts. This mixed-media project is a bit more involved than some of the other projects. The volcano will need to dry for a few days, so plan ahead. To simplify, you could skip the volcano. But if you're ready to show off a truly magnificent terrarium, start by making the volcano. A few days later, once the volcano is dry, build the terrarium. Then put it all together for hours of imaginative play. When you're ready for high drama, gather the family and let it blow!

TOY TALK

TOP TOYS: A sauropod such as a *Brontosaurus* or *Brachiosaurus*
SUBSTITUTES: Any toy dinosaurs of your choice

MATERIALS & TOOLS

FOR THE TERRARIUM:

1 rectangular container (a large pan with a lip works well)

1 Papier-Mâché Volcano (optional; see page 93 for activity)

Black aquarium gravel or black sand

Black rocks, pebbles, and/or small stones

Preserved sheet moss, reindeer moss, and/or pillow moss

2 or 3 plants, in original plastic containers or potted in small glass jelly jars (optional; see "Mini Dino Terrariums," page 109, for quick tutorial)

Decorations of your choice: sand, tiny pebbles, sticks, seedlings, pine cones, rocks, leaves

Toy dinosaur(s), miniature size

FOR THE ERUPTION:

White vinegar

Red food dye

Baking soda

Small pitcher or liquid measuring cup (something that has a spout for easy pouring)

Funnel

Long-handled spoon or skewer (to stir up a second eruption)

DIRECTIONS

1. If you plan to include a homemade volcano, start with "Papier-Mâché Volcano," page 93. Allow time for the volcano to dry. If you want to skip the volcano, proceed to the next step to create a gorgeous end-of-the-world habitat.

2. Wash and dry your container. If you've already made a volcano, place it in the container. Is it sitting at the right height compared to the edge? If not, remove the volcano and add a thin layer of black gravel or sand. Once you're happy with the height and position of your volcano, pour black gravel or sand around the base to blend the volcano into the scene. If you are not including a volcano, simply fill the container with a layer of black sand or gravel.

3. Build the landscape, adding any natural features you like—a pond, a stream, a forest, a beach, a mountain, you name it! Try using blue stones or beads to create water, or large black rocks draped in green sheet moss to form mountains.

4. If you'd like to include plants, they will need individual containers since this terrarium doesn't include soil. You'll also need to protect them from the vinegar in the eruption, which will hurt them. Slip each plant (still in its original plastic container) into a slightly larger container that doesn't have a drainage hole, or remove plastic containers and transplant into glass jelly jars (see "Mini Dino Terrariums," page 109). If you're not including a volcano, you could simply set the plants (in their original plastic containers) directly into the scene.

5. Use more black sand, along with green sheet moss, to hide the plant containers and blend the plants into the landscape. Layer moss over the base of your volcano or around the edges of the container to create hills or cliffs.

6. Set your titanosaurs into the terrarium.

7. Enjoy your terrarium as it is. It's stunning! Or if you'd like to act out a dramatic end to the Cretaceous Period, invite over some friends and get ready for some major excitement!

If you choose to stage a real eruption, make sure you're working outside or on a protected surface. Red dye stains clothes, so wear a smock or old play clothes. Have the camera ready. This is going to go fast!

- First, mix the vinegar with red food dye in the small pitcher.

- Next, pour baking soda into the volcano cup. Use a funnel if the opening is small.

- *Stop.* Is everyone watching? When you have everyone's attention, pour the red vinegar into the hole and stand back. Here comes a giant river of red lava!

Papier-Mâché Volcano

Have you ever worked with papier-mâché? If not, get ready to let your creativity shine. Once you have the technique down, you can make one-of-a-kind piñatas for all your parties. This project is extra special because the volcano doesn't just look cool. It will actually erupt! Allow several days for your volcano to dry completely before adding it to your dino world. Also, be aware that the eruption may destroy the volcano, unless you pour off the "lava" and allow it to dry out again right away.

MATERIALS & TOOLS

Newspaper

1 cup flour, plus more as needed

Water

1 disposable water bottle or a narrow paper or plastic cup

1 paper plate or a circle cut out of cardboard

Scissors

Masking tape

Paint and paintbrush

TIP: This is a messy job, so work outside or protect your work surface with lots of newspaper. Also, be sure to allow several days for the finished volcano to dry before painting. Then plan on another day or two for the paint to dry.

DIRECTIONS

1. Tear or cut the newspaper into strips about 1 to 2 inches wide. You will need a big stack of strips. Your hands will be covered in paste later on, so make more than you think you'll need. Compost or recycle any leftovers.

2. Whisk together 1 cup of flour and 2 cups of water in a large mixing bowl until you get a smooth, runny paste (like thin pancake batter). Mix up more paste as needed, using 1 part flour to 2 parts water.

3. Tape the water bottle or cup to the paper plate or piece of cardboard, to add stability. You can tape some crumpled-up newspapers under the cup for added height. Crumple up some newspaper and tape it around the cup or bottle to form a volcano shape. Make sure not to cover over the mouth of the container. Dip both sides of each newspaper strip in the paste. Wrap the wet strips around the newspaper shape, connecting any gaps and crisscrossing the strips in different directions. Smooth, press, and shape with your fingers as you go. Layer more wet strips until you get a sturdy volcano shape you like. You can make the opening more narrow, but don't cover it completely.

4. Allow the volcano to dry completely. This will take at least 24 to 48 hours, even longer in a humid climate.

5. Paint the volcano whatever colors you like (black, gray, or green at the bottom; red at the top). Allow to dry completely, until hard to the touch.

BIG BOOM:
ASTEROID EXPERIMENT

Volcanic eruptions in India and climate change probably played a role in the dinosaurs' extinction. But most paleontologists believe that the primary cause was the asteroid impact in the area of modern-day Mexico that left behind a crater more than a hundred miles across. After 66 million years, we can't see the asteroid on the surface, but we use special instruments to see where it hit. We can also find evidence of it in many places in the rock record, including tiny droplets of natural glass and concentrations of a rare chemical element. You can measure the impact of a giant asteroid with this fun experiment.

MATERIALS & TOOLS

Large tub or container

Play sand or flour

Colored play sand (optional)

Several balls of different sizes and shapes (marble, golf ball, tennis ball, etc.)

Piece of paper

Pen or pencil

Ruler

DIRECTIONS

1. Carefully pour play sand or flour into a tub and smooth the surface. If you like, sprinkle a thin layer of colored sand on top.

2. Take a tennis ball and drop it into the sand. Notice the size and shape of the impact. Next, have someone taller than you drop it. Or stand on a chair to get up higher. Now try it with a golf ball or marble. (If you use flour, it's best to do this activity outside!)

3. Notice the different kinds of craters you've created. How are they different? If you used a layer of colored sand, how did the impact change the two layers? Did you end up with a big dust cloud? Did the weight of the "asteroid" change the impact?

4. To take your experiment to the next level, make a chart of your findings! On a piece of paper, write down each type of "asteroid" (marble, golf ball, tennis ball, etc.). Use a measuring stick to measure the sizes of the different "asteroid" impacts. Record the size and characteristics of each "crater" in your chart.

5. Based on what you noticed in your experiment and chart, ask yourself: What kind of problems would a huge crater cause for life on Earth?

Another fun idea would be to grab some large balls (basketball, football) and try this experiment outside in a sandbox in your backyard or at your local playground.

DINO DIG

Aardonyx to Zuul

ROCKS AT A GLANCE

GROUP	HOW FORMED	EXAMPLES	FOSSILS?
Igneous	Cooling lava (at Earth's surface) Cooling magma (deep beneath the surface)	Basalt (from lava) Gabbro (from magma) Granite (from magma)	No; nothing lives in lava or magma
Metamorphic	Igneous or sedimentary rocks exposed to great heat or pressure	Gneiss Marble Schist Slate	Rare; metamorphism destroys most fossils
Sedimentary	Accumulations of particles (sand, silt, pebbles, crystals)	Limestone Sandstone Shale	Yes; some sedimentary rocks are almost entirely fossils

PALEONTOLOGISTS
AT WORK

People have found dinosaur fossils all over the world, from Antarctica to north of the Arctic Circle. Although many finds have been accidental, paleontologists don't just sit around and wait for lucky finds. They go out and find dinosaurs themselves! But how do they figure out where to look for dinosaurs?

Understanding geology is key. Geologic maps show where various kinds of rock are found at the surface. This is important because fossils are only found in certain rocks (see "Rocks at a Glance," page 97). You'll also want to look in rocks of the right age. Rocks that are too old may have marine fossils but no dinosaurs. If the rocks are too young, you may find abundant mammals instead. And people can't just dig for fossils anywhere. Once paleontologists choose an area that might have dinosaurs, they must first get permission to look for fossils there.

Often the best rocks for finding dinosaurs are in areas where few people live. After all, rocks are best exposed in places with little plant cover, roads, or buildings. If the land won't support plants or soil, people won't want to live there either. This is why many dinosaur expeditions are in remote areas. Careful planning is necessary to pack tools, food, water, tents, and first-aid supplies for the trip because you can't run to a store when you are out in the middle of nowhere. A dinosaur dig is a lot like camping!

Finding fossils is usually about walking around, looking at the ground. Some fossils can be collected without a lot of help, but if you find large bones or bonebeds, you'll need the whole crew. Digging is hard, backbreaking work—especially because many dinosaur digs are in very hot areas. Dinosaur diggers have to protect themselves from sunburn, heat stroke, snakes, and injuries. But all the work is worth it when they find a great dinosaur fossil.

When you remove a fossil, you'll want to do two things. First, you'll want to protect the fossil so that it can be moved (see "How to Dig and Collect a Dinosaur Bone," page 99). Second, you'll want to document the fossil's surroundings. Good paleontologists take photographs and careful notes as they work. If there are many fossils in a small area, you'll make a quarry map that shows where each one was found. You'll also want to record information such as the kind of rock and other kinds of fossils found there. This information will help you and other scientists describe what kind of environment the dinosaur lived in.

Once the fossils have been sent to a museum, people called preparators get them ready for study. They remove the rock sticking to the bones, clean up any skin impressions, glue together broken pieces, and apply chemicals to strengthen the fossils. If the rock is hard or the bones are fragmentary, this can take years of very delicate work.

After the fossils have been prepared, dinosaurs can be studied carefully. Some dinosaur fossils are mounted in museums for people to see. Other fossils go into storage in museum collections, where researchers can study them. Maybe one day you'll be one of those researchers!

HOW TO DIG AND COLLECT A DINOSAUR BONE

1. Figure out the size of the fossil.

2. Dig around the sides, but not too close—if you keep some of the rock surrounding it, the fossil will be stronger.

3. Cover the top and sides with material such as plaster and burlap to make a protective shell.

4. When the shell is ready, carefully dig under the fossil so you can "pop" it from the rock.

5. Flip it over and plaster the bottom like you did the top. It's ready to go!

LOST IN THE MUSEUM

Fossils in museum collections are sometimes misidentified or set aside because no one working there is an expert on that kind of fossil. Visiting scientists sometimes rediscover these fossils and identify them. Every so often, one of these overlooked fossils turns out to be something that was unknown, and it gets described in a scientific journal.

Utah Dinosaur Dig

One of the world's best places to find dinosaur fossils is the state of Utah. Home to the Morrison Formation, this area is famous for its bizarre red rock formations and Dinosaur National Monument. It looks like Mars! Hulking red-rock towers, natural arches, and weird hoodoos (crinkly columns of rock) decorate the landscape. One day you might be lucky enough to hike one of the slot canyons of Grand Staircase-Escalante and explore this wonder of the world for yourself. In the meantime, let's build a dinosaur dig complete with red-rock formations, tents, and pickup trucks. Don't forget to bury lots of dinosaur bones for those hard-working paleontologists to dig up!

TOY TALK

TOP TOYS: Dinosaur skeleton miniature toys (any dinosaur) and other miniature toys (paleontologist figures, pickup truck, map, tent, shovel, ice pick, dustpan, brush)
SUBSTITUTES: Any miniature toy dinosaurs

MATERIALS & TOOLS

1 wide, shallow container

Plain play sand

Toy dinosaur skeletons

Miniature toys such as a pickup truck, dustpan, shovel, ice pick, or paintbrush

Decorations of your choice: large red-rock slabs, tiny pebbles, sticks, seedlings, pine cones, rocks, blue stones, leaves

Colored sand in reddish tones (red, orange, coral, pink)

2 or 3 air plants (see "Plant Picks," page 102)

Scissors (optional)

DIRECTIONS

1. Fill your container with a thick layer of play sand.

2. Bury the skeleton sets intact, or have an adult cut them up with sharp scissors. Lay out the bones in a pile for the paleontologists to untangle, then cover with sand.

3. Using larger stones or more pebbles, create any geological features you like. Remember, Utah is famous for its massive red-rock formations. What about a canyon, a cliff, or a cave—or even an arch? Tilt large red rocks upright to form canyon walls. Sprinkle swirls of reddish sand over the foundation to create the famous red-rock glow of Utah. Get the sand wet and you can even make hoodoos or slot canyons.

4. Place the air plants on the surface of the play sand.

5. Roll in with the trucks, ice picks, and dustpans, and get those paleontologists to work digging up fossils! Who will make the next big discovery?

PLANT PICKS

It may seem that no plant or animal could survive the harsh conditions of the Utah desert, but look again! Have you ever seen red rock country in the springtime? Cacti and wildflowers bloom with abundant yellow and orange flowers. In winter, the desert landscape may seem stark and empty, but even then, if you look closely, you will find signs of life all around you. When you pick out air plants for your dino dig, choose ones that resemble common Utah desert plants such as sagebrush, prickly pear cactus, scrub live oak, and creosote bush. See "Plant Doctor," page 6, for suggestions on how to keep your air plants healthy. If you choose to use homemade colored sand made of salt (see "Colored Sand" recipe variation, page 50), make sure the salt doesn't touch any air plants.

TRUE OR FALSE?

Dinosaur bones can be found under the sea.

Answer: True. The sauropod *Histriasaurus* is known from bones discovered in rocks at the bottom of the Adriatic Sea just off the coast of Croatia. How do you think paleontologists dig up underwater fossils?

Fossil Impression with Homemade Modeling Clay

There's nothing more fun than playing with dough. But have you ever made dough with glue? This recipe makes a stiff, elastic dough that will harden into a firm clay. It's perfect for creating fossil impressions.

MATERIALS & TOOLS

Nontoxic school glue

Cornstarch

Flour

Play sand or beach sand (optional)

Toy dinosaurs

Decorations of your choice: pine cones, leaves, insect toys, shells, sticks

Paint and paintbrush (optional)

DIRECTIONS

1. Mix together equal parts glue, cornstarch, and flour in a bowl.

2. Knead until you have a smooth, thick, elastic modeling clay.

3. Pull off pieces and roll into balls. Press into disks.

4. Generously dust your disks and your chosen dinosaurs with cornstarch or sand, to prevent sticking. Stamp your dinosaurs into the clay, pressing firmly to leave a deep impression. Try using just their feet or their whole bodies. Push in any decorations that you choose.

5. Allow to dry. Brush off any loose cornstarch or sand. Paint if desired. You made a fossil impression!

DEEPEST DINO DIG

Plateosaurus bones have been found in rock cored from more than 7,400 feet beneath the North Sea, where thick layers of sediment had buried them over the past 200 million years.

PARTY TIME

How to Throw a Dino-Tastic Gathering

Birthday party around the corner? Need a unique activity for preschool? Rainy Saturday afternoon stuck inside and running out of ideas fast? This is the chapter for you! Pick and choose from these activities and recipes to put together a full-blown dino birthday party, complete with a volcano ice cream cake and dinosaur ice eggs. Or plan a simple terrarium-building activity for your Boy Scouts den or after-school playdate. With a little bit of prep, you can lead a simple but unforgettable dino project. Creating something with our hands puts a smile on everyone's face. Put on some music, pull out the streamers, and get ready to party!

Mini Dino Terrariums

For this project, it's a good idea to set up a workspace ahead of time. Make stations for each guest, being sure to set out all the materials they'll need. Who needs party favors when your friends can take home their own tiny dino world?

MATERIALS & TOOLS

Widemouthed (4-ounce) jelly jars, lids removed, 1 per person

Miniature dinosaur toys, 1 per person

Miniature plants, 1 per person (see "Modern Plant Look-Alikes," page xxi)

Wooden popsicle sticks or spoons, 1 per person

Decorations of your choice: small shells, sticks, seedpods, stones, large glass beads

Pea gravel or aquarium gravel

Potting soil

Bowls and scoops for shared materials

DIRECTIONS

1. For each person, set up a station with a jar, a dinosaur toy, a plant, and a popsicle stick or spoon. In the middle of the table, set out bowls of gravel, potting soil, and decorations, along with scoops. Make sure everyone can reach the shared materials.

2. Tell your guests what you've learned about prehistoric plants. Ferns and mosses are always a great choice. Shamrock looks like a prehistoric ginkgo and miniature parlor palms resemble cycads. Horsetail is one of the world's oldest living land plants.

3. Teach your guests a simplified version (skip the charcoal and perlite) of the layer cake method you used for the bigger terrariums in this book. Start by adding a thin layer of gravel to the jar. Remove the plastic liner and position your plant, then add potting soil around the edges. Press down lightly with your fingers or popsicle stick to get rid of air pockets, and add more potting soil as needed. Then add other decorations of your choice. Don't forget your dino toy!

TIP: If you can't find widemouthed 4-ounce jars, take a peek in your recycling bin. You might find other containers there!

Dinosaur Ice Eggs

For this activity, know that if you include mallets, they will be the star of the show. Every kid will be banging on those eggs with all their might. If you have a big group and all that hammering sounds chaotic, skip the mallets and let your guests use their observation skills to experiment with the power of water, salt, and patience. Observation and patience? The paleontologists approve.

MATERIALS & TOOLS

Miniature dinosaur toys, 1 per person
(plus a few extras)

Balloons

Decorations of your choice: flowers,
grass, sticks, tiny shells

Basket lined with grass clippings or
hay (to look like a "nest")

Bowls of hot water

Bowls of kosher salt or a salt shaker

Tools: syringes, turkey baster, eyedroppers,
toothbrushes, wooden mallets, popsicle sticks,
spoons, butter knives (for older kids)

DIRECTIONS

1. A day or two before your event, carefully stretch out a balloon and squeeze a miniature dinosaur toy inside. It helps to have two people for this job! Don't worry. You'll only pop a few balloons. Add any other tiny decorative objects of your choice. Fill the balloon with water and tie it closed. (If you want to make big eggs, fill the balloons with a garden hose.)

2. Lay the balloon eggs in a single layer on a cookie sheet and freeze overnight, or until completely solid. Once hardened, cut off tops of the balloons and peel off.

3. Set up a workspace for your experiment. Line your surface with thick craft paper or newspaper. Set out the bowls of hot water, bowls of salt, and various tools. Lay the ice eggs in a basket lined with grass or hay.

4. Have each guest choose an egg. Tell them to experiment with which tools work best! Squirt the eggs with warm water, scratch with salt, or tap and chip away to reveal the dinosaurs hidden inside.

Sew a Dino Card

This is a fun project for kids of all ages. It's also great for hand-eye coordination and fine motor skills. If you set this up as a party activity, be sure to prepare a few samples ahead of time. Ask a crafty adult or older child to help the younger kids.

MATERIALS & TOOLS

Heavy card stock (old calendars also work well)

Yarn

Hole punch

Tapestry needles with blunt points

Scissors

DIRECTIONS

1. Trace or print a very simple outline of a dinosaur onto the card stock and cut out the shape. The simpler the better. (For very young children, cut out a square or circle with a picture or stamp of a dinosaur in the center.) Use the hole punch to punch a border of holes around the edge. Repeat until you have enough cards for each guest.

2. Make up a sample to display at the party. Try one of these stitches:

   - **Straight stitch:** Cut a long piece of yarn (longer than you think you'll need but not so long that it's unmanageable). Thread the needle. Pick a hole and come up from the back side of the card to the front. Pull the yarn through until you have a 3-inch tail. Using the fingers of your nondominant hand, hold the tail against the back of the card until you've completed a few stitches. Thread down through the next hole. Repeat this up-and-down stitch all the way around. On the back of the card, tie together with your tail (or tuck under stitches) and trim.

   - **Straight stitch without gaps:** The basic straight stitch will create gaps between stitches. If you want to create a continuous line of stitches, be sure to punch an odd number of holes. Allow double the yarn length and do a straight stitch all the way around twice. The second time around, you'll close up the gaps from the first pass.

   - **Overcast stitch:** Cut a long piece of yarn and thread the needle. Pick a hole and come up from the back side of the card to the front. Pull the yarn through until you have a 3-inch tail. Pinch the tail in your nondominant hand, then take the needle around the outside edge of the card to the back of the next hole, coming up to the front again. Repeat all the way around the edge. Tie off on the back side, or tuck under. Trim.

Sandbox Dino Dig

There's nothing more exciting than digging for treasure—especially when it's dino treasure!
This simple activity might just steal the show.

MATERIALS & TOOLS

Outdoor sandbox or a large tub
filled with play sand

Miniature dinosaur skeleton toys (enough
for each guest to find at least 3 or 4)

Shovels or scoops

Toy dump trucks (optional)

DIRECTIONS

Before your party (or while no one is looking), dig
holes in the sand and hide the dinosaur skeletons.
When it's time for the dino dig, give each child a
scoop or shovel and let them take a turn digging for
dino treasure.

Dino Stamp Wrapping Paper

Did you know you can make your own wrapping paper? Grab some dinosaur stamps and get stamping!

MATERIALS & TOOLS

Roll of wide craft paper (natural or white) or plain muslin fabric

Dinosaur rubber stamps

Ink pads

DIRECTIONS

Working on a large, flat surface such as a dining room table (or the floor if it's not too dirty!), lay out your craft paper or fabric. You may want to weight the edges with some canned goods or a bean bag. Stamp away. Let dry, then use as wrapping paper.

Volcano Ice Cream Cake

Serves 16-20

Everyone loves ice cream cake—especially one with a chocolate cookie base layer, a soil layer made of ice cream, a volcano with strawberry "lava," and dinosaur figures! Use your imagination to create a dino landscape made out of crushed cookies, ice cream, whipped cream, and chocolate sauce. Don't forget to add miniature dinosaurs, trees, or boulders. This homemade birthday cake will wow all your party guests. It looks and tastes amazing! The secret? It's actually super simple to make. You need to start it a day ahead, but most of the prep involves sticking it in the freezer and walking away. Now that's a birthday cake everyone can enjoy. Happy Birthday!

INGREDIENTS

1 (20-ounce) package chocolate sandwich cookies

½ cup (1 stick) butter, melted

2 (1.75 quart) containers ice cream
(flavor of your choice)

1 (16-ounce) container chocolate sauce
(or 2 cups homemade)

1 pint fresh or 1 (10-ounce) bag frozen strawberries or raspberries (defrosted, if frozen)

2 tablespoons sugar (optional, depending on sweetness of berries)

1 teaspoon fresh lemon juice (optional)

1 cup heavy cream, cold

1 tablespoon confectioners' sugar
(more or less, depending on your taste)

½ teaspoon vanilla

Dinosaur toys, washed

Miniature plastic trees or other decorations of your choice, washed

Sprinkles, crushed cookies, or chopped macadamia nuts (optional)

Birthday candles

TOOLS & EQUIPMENT

One 9 x 13-inch baking pan or casserole dish, freezer-safe

Food processor

Standing mixer or electric beaters

Small pitcher

TIP: Make this dessert (up until the chocolate syrup layer) a day or two before your event so it has plenty of time to freeze.

DIRECTIONS

1. In a food processor, pulse the cookies into crumbs. Add the melted butter and pulse until the crumbs start to clump together. Dump into a 9 x 13-inch pan. (The cake will be served in this container, so choose one you like.) Press firmly to make an even crust. Freeze for at least 30 minutes.

2. If your ice cream comes in rectangular cardboard containers, take off the lid, then use scissors to cut the cardboard away from the block of ice cream. Set the hunk of ice cream on a cutting board and, using a large knife, slice into

thick slabs. Layer the slabs on top of the cookie crust, sealing any cracks with a spatula or wooden spoon. Working quickly before the ice cream melts, create a volcano shape out of ice cream. Cover with foil, tenting the foil to avoid the volcano. Freeze at least 30 minutes.

3. Spread the chocolate sauce evenly over the ice cream, avoiding the volcano. Cover with foil and freeze for at least 12 hours.

4. Prepare the lava by pureeing the berries, sugar (if needed), and lemon juice in a blender or food processor until smooth. Place in a small attractive pitcher, cover, and refrigerate until ready to serve.

5. Before serving, beat the cold heavy cream together with the confectioners' sugar and vanilla until peaks form. Spread on top of the cake. Decorate the cake with mini dinosaurs and trees, sprinkles, crushed cookies, nuts, birthday candles, or any other items of your choice. Serve immediately or return to the freezer. (Be aware that the whipped topping will get a slightly icy texture if kept in the freezer for hours. Also, for easier slicing, allow the cake to thaw at room temperature for about 15 minutes before serving.)

6. When you're ready to present the cake, get everyone's attention. Pour the berry lava over the volcano and watch it spill over the landscape. (Serve separately for picky eaters.) To cut clean layers, dip a sharp knife in hot water. Enjoy!

HOW TO THROW A PARTY AND ENJOY IT TOO

Remember the days when birthdays meant Mom served your favorite meal and maybe a homemade cake or store-bought ice cream to share with your family? Were you disappointed? No. Let's relax with the wedding-level planning (and spending) on kids' birthdays! Parents, please give yourself permission to dial it down.

Spread out a blanket and read a picture book about dinosaurs. Play an old-fashioned party game: pin-the-tail-on-the-dinosaur never gets old; duck, duck, goose—you know, the classics. Share some homemade cake, a basket of blueberries, or a bowl of frozen yogurt. Laugh. Go slow. Choose and protect simplicity.

Here are a few tried-and-true strategies for a beautiful, personal gathering that doesn't leave everyone depleted:

CHOOSE YOUR OWN ADVENTURE

Don't rely on prepackaged Disney characters to provide your party theme. You don't need to book a magic show, buy a designer cake, rent a bounce house, or hire a party planner. If you want to do those things, great. But is it really necessary? Think for yourself. Resist materialism, clutter, and over-whelm. Start simple. Pick a theme or activity your child adores. Think dinosaurs, elephants, trucks, fairies, camping—whatever your unique, beautiful child is excited about right now.

TRIM THE GUEST LIST

You don't need to invite every child in your kid's class. This isn't a popularity contest. How old is your child turning? That's how many friends they can invite. Young children can't handle fifteen guests and their loitering parents. After an hour

of overstimulation, the birthday boy or girl will be crying in the corner. You'll be sweaty and stressed, your house will be a wreck, and you'll have set the bar so impossibly high that kids can't enjoy the simple, quiet pleasures of life.

START WITH WHITE

Start collecting simple white tablecloths. These are so versatile. "White?" you may be asking. "Really?" Well, guess what? If they get dirty or smeared with chocolate sauce (which means it was a good party!), toss them in the washer with a good stain remover and they'll be back in shape for your next event.

ROTATE IN COLOR

Pick two (max three) complementary colors for your party. Make sure all your decorations—streamers, table runners, yarn in dino cards, napkins, signs— all match that color scheme. That way you create instant color unity, which is soothing to the eye and creates a cohesive look for your event. Buy or sew simple runners and napkins in bright colors and patterns to throw on top of your basic white tablecloth. Voilà! A fresh new party look, but you didn't have to a purchase a brand-new, once-and-done, pricey tablecloth that will now gather dust in the closet.

SIGNS

Print or write out a simple welcome message in a fun font on a piece of card stock. Punch a hole in each of the top corners and thread with coordinating ribbon. Hang it on your front door to help guests feel welcome. Print out another message related to your party theme (in the same font) and pop it into a white frame. Prop it up next to a name tag station or one of your gorgeous dinosaur terrariums. Again, instant coziness for your guests.

SKIP THE PLASTIC

Why not ditch the plastic cups and instead use glass mason jars? Pop in a paper straw (in one of your party colors) and set them out on a white tray for a festive splash of color. Buy a glass beverage dispenser at a yard sale or thrift store. Fill it with lemonade and a few slices of lemon, or water with strawberries and ice. So much prettier and healthier than a cooler of juice boxes. After a few parties, that glass dispenser and those mason jars will have paid for themselves. I don't know about you, but my favorite parties are the ones where there's essentially zero trash. No dumping junk in landfills, no blowing the family budget. Sounds good to me!

CENTER DOWN

Stop all prep 2 hours before your party. Take a walk, shower, get yourself ready, drink some water, eat a heathy snack. Meanwhile, let the birthday child listen to an audiobook in a quiet room or have someone take them on a quick bike ride around the neighborhood to burn off nervous energy. Once you're dressed and they're calm, then help your child get dressed. Put on some music and finish any last-minute tasks. If the host looks frazzled and the birthday boy or girl is amped up, guests will feel it and no one will be able to relax.

EMBRACE IMPERFECTION

Parties are meant to celebrate joy and real, messy connection. Let go of that Instagram vision of unattainable perfection. Don't worry about cleaning your bedroom. Don't vacuum. The floors will get dirty at the party anyway! Choose a few details that are important to you, then give yourself full permission to ditch the rest. Put on your favorite tunes and spend a couple of minutes watching your child's face. Give them a hug. Slow down so you can truly savor this milestone with your child and the friends and family who love them!

ACKNOWLEDGMENTS

Like all good things, this book is a labor of love and community. I am forever grateful to the smart, imaginative kids who inspired me with project ideas and terrarium designs, regaled me with dinosaur facts, and bluntly informed me when ideas weren't "cool." Huge, heartfelt gratitude to all those who served as builders, models, and idea generators: Jack Kortsch, Owen Kortsch, Townsend Herbst, Ellory Herbst, Marin Herbst, Janis Herbst, Amaris Perez, Gavin Perez, Milena Lopez, Wonenouon Somé, Eli Schock, Sage Schock, Kenzie Williamson, Sebastian Williamson, Lily Flaherty, Oliver Flaherty, Noah Shurz, Seth Shurz, Ava Carter, Zephaniah Carter, Isabelle Gallagher, Graham Gallagher, Carol Kortsch, and Skylar Rose. Ms. Alicia Ruiz's fourth-grade class at Denver Language School provided fantastic questions for the paleontologist interview.

Thank you to my family and friends for putting up with terrarium and photography talk at every turn. Special thanks goes to my mother, Karen Bayles, a lifelong early childhood educator, and my mother-in-law, Carol Kortsch, a master gardener, for expert recommendations. Christine Chitnis, a veteran Roost author, offered sage advice early in the project, and my friend Jonalee Earles, a lifestyle and wedding photographer, talked me through some photography tips. Huge gratitude to Ali DeJohn, founder of The Makerie retreats, who supported my crazy idea to combine creative writing with succulent container design and gave me a teaching job. I would not have started my Ink & Stem Workshops without her belief in my creative soul. To all my students—college students, Denver Botanic Gardens students, and Ink & Stem students: thank you for inspiring me with your fierce creativity.

Gardens and wild places are my favorites, so researching and creating projects for this book was a delight. For inspiration during the research process, special thanks to the Denver Botanic Gardens, City Floral Garden Center (Denver, Colorado), Wild Flowers (Denver, Colorado), Roosevelt's Terrariums (Portland, Oregon), New York Botanical Garden, Chanticleer Garden (Wayne, Pennsylvania), and the Heller Garden of Gardone Riviera (Brescia, Italy). Many ideas in this book were inspired by the extravagant beauty of wild nature in Colorado, Utah, the Pacific Northwest, Vermont, North Carolina, Italy, Tulum (Mexico), and Muskoka (Ontario, Canada).

This book would not exist without the hard work and collaborative spirit of Justin Tweet and Dr. Karen Chin. Their expertise and passion for the project made them a joy to work with. The idea for this book came from my talented editor at Roost Books, Juree Sondker. When Juree approached me with the idea for a dinosaur terrarium book, I was quickly entranced by her warmth and creative vision. Her unflagging enthusiasm made working on the book a pleasure from start to finish. Thank you to Kristen Hatgi Sink (and her assistant, Kate Wilker), who captured the magic of the projects in the incredible chapter cover shots. I had so much fun working on our photo shoots! Huge thanks to the fantastic team at Roost Books, especially Breanna Locke, Daniel Urban-Brown, Kara Plikaitis, Sara Bercholz, Claire Kelley, and Jess Townsend, and the freelance editors Mollie Firestone and Emily Wichland. My shelves have been stuffed with beautiful Roost Books for many years; to publish my own book with Roost is truly a dream come true.

My brilliant children, Jack and Owen Kortsch, have been invaluable contributors to every single step of this project. They are my daily joy and the reason behind it all. A huge shout-out to my husband, Daniel Kortsch, whose unfailing support, photography expertise, listening ear, and mad skills with papier-mâché made this project possible. I promise to clean up all the terrariums now.

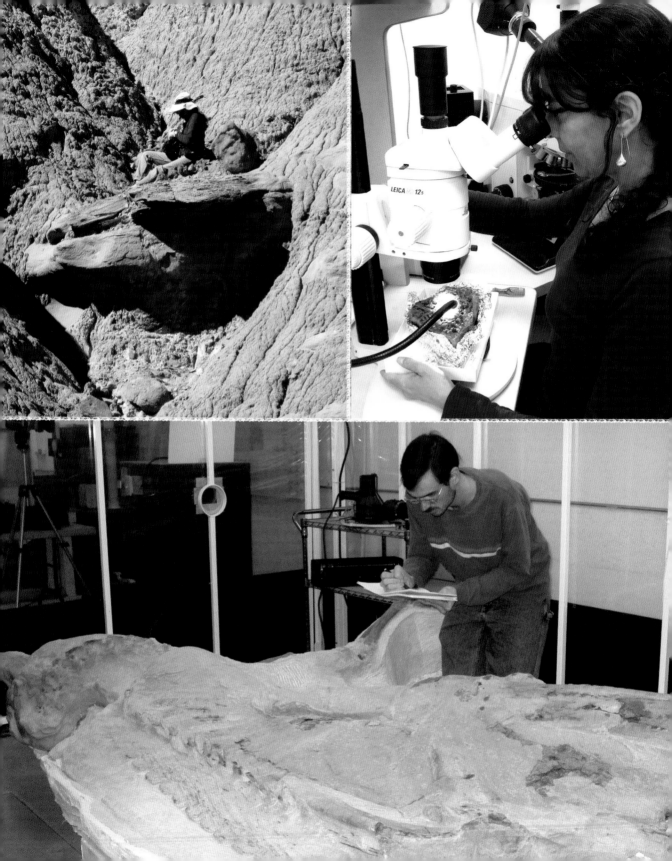

INTERVIEW
Kids Ask...

Questions for Dr. Karen Chin and Justin Tweet from Alicia Ruiz's fourth-grade class at Denver Language School, Denver, Colorado

When did you know you wanted to be a paleontologist when you grew up?

Justin: I'm not sure when I decided to commit to a career (it started coming together in high school), but I was "bit by the bug" when I was five. I had been really interested in astronomy, but I drifted away when I found out we couldn't actually go anywhere because we couldn't go faster than the speed of light. Why I picked dinosaurs after that I don't know now, but I do know that what sealed it was getting *The Illustrated Encyclopedia of Dinosaurs* for Christmas 1986.

Karen: My journey toward becoming a paleontologist was somewhat unusual because I did not choose this career path until I was an adult. In fact, I did not understand why anyone would want to study dinosaurs or other extinct animals when they could learn about the wonderful animals that are alive today. All that changed after I got a job preparing dinosaur bones for dinosaur paleontologist Jack Horner. After that, I was hooked and could not learn

enough about dinosaurs and the environments they lived in. I find it incredibly exciting to try to answer questions about ancient ecosystems! I still love learning about the wonderful animals that are alive today, but now I study living animals to help me understand ancient life.

How can you tell if the dinosaur was male or female?

Justin: Most times you can't. However, we know that living female birds form a special tissue in their bones when they are laying eggs, and this same kind of tissue has been found in dinosaur bones. The hard part is the tissue is inside the bone, so you have to cut it open to see it or have a bone that's broken just right.

Do you ever search for fossils underwater?

Justin: I've never searched directly underwater, but I have looked for shark teeth along beaches, so I've gotten close! (Once I fell in, but then I was

133

more interested in getting out of the water than looking for fossils.)

Which dinosaur is the biggest that you've encountered?

Justin: When I work at the Science Museum of Minnesota, I'm often in a collections vault where there are many bones of *Diplodocus* and other sauropods. The biggest dinosaur I've personally worked with, though, was Leonardo the *Brachylophosaurus*, which was only half grown, maybe 20 feet or so long.

Karen: I once helped dig up an articulated *Tyrannosaurus rex* skeleton in Montana. That was one massive and very cool dinosaur!

How do you know where to search for the dinosaurs?

Justin: The most important tools are geologic maps and papers that other paleontologists have written. With geologic maps I can search for places where the right kinds of rocks are exposed, and with the scientific papers I can find if anyone else has found fossils in those places before.

In what place have you found the most dinosaur bones?

Justin: I live and work in Minnesota, where we've only found fewer than a half dozen dinosaur bones in the whole state. However, there are lots and lots of fossils of marine animals that lived long before the dinosaurs, about 455 million years ago. I can find rocks that are almost entirely made of tiny pieces of seashells, snails, trilobites, sea lilies, and other similar fossils. It's much easier for seashells to become fossils than dinosaurs because they're smaller, more abundant, and easier to bury!

Karen: I have discovered dinosaur bones and other dinosaur fossils in Montana, Utah, and New Mexico. I have also been lucky enough to visit other dinosaur quarries in North Dakota, Colorado, Wyoming, Texas, Canada, and Mexico.

What tools do you use for digging up the dinosaur bones?

Justin: I've mostly worked with small marine fossils, which usually only need hands (or gloves), a toothbrush, water, and sometimes dental tools to collect and prepare.

Karen: The most important tools I use to dig up dinosaur bones are ice picks, paintbrushes, and dustpans. We use small tools when we are digging around bones because we don't want to damage the fossils. But we can use shovels or picks if we aren't digging right next to fossil bones.

Where do you put the bones after you dig them up?

Justin: When I visit a national park for my work, most of the fossils I find are left in the ground for the public to enjoy. If I collect something, it becomes part of the park's collections, or it goes to a museum that the park partners with.

Karen: Dinosaur fossils are taken to museums so that they can be stored properly and other paleontologists can study them.

Why do you like to do your job?

Justin: I work for the National Park Service, and I get to keep track of fossils and fossil information for more than 270 parks (and counting) from Maine to Alaska. I get to work with everything from billion-year-old microbial mats to mammoth and sloth fossils from just after the last Ice Age. When I was a student, I had trouble deciding what I wanted to focus on. Now I don't have to choose!

Karen: The best part of my job is making new paleontological discoveries about ancient life. I made some of these discoveries while I was hunting for fossils in the field and others when examining fossils with a microscope in my laboratory.

What was your favorite discovery?

Justin: My favorite discovery is a rare fossil of a small marine animal called a conulariid, which looked kind of like a coral living in a four-sided ice cream cone made up of tiny stacked rods. I found it in a city park, so I left it in place, and now I can see it anytime I visit.

Karen: My favorite discovery was finding dung beetle burrows in dinosaur coprolites (fossilized feces). This means that big dinosaurs and small dung beetles were ecological partners some 75 million years ago.

Where is your favorite place to look for bones?

Justin: I don't get to look for bones very often where I am. However, I can go out to places around Minneapolis and St. Paul and see all kinds of marine fossils. My favorite place is a park called Shadow Falls near the Mississippi. It's a city park, so I leave the fossils where they are, but I can hike around in the bluffs and see things I've never seen before.

Karen: My favorite places to look for dinosaur bones are Montana, Utah, and Colorado.

Who was the first person to find a bone?

Justin: We don't know! People have been finding fossils for as long as there have been people, but it's only been since the late 1700s that we've begun to understand fossils for what they are. You might say that the first dinosaur bones were bits and pieces of *Megalosaurus* and *Iguanodon* found in England in the late 1700s and early 1800s, because they were the main fossils used to create the word "dinosaur" in 1842.

How many times have you thought you found dinosaur bones, but then you discover they're actually dog bones or something?

Justin: Some fossils can look a lot like other kinds of fossils. When I worked on Leonardo, I spent a lot of time trying to figure out if what I thought were burrows inside the body were actually left by plant roots. The closest I've ever come to what you describe was when some people I was working with had a little fossil that I thought might be a fish backbone, but when we got a better look at it, it turned out to be a kind of shell called a brachiopod. Sometimes I'm asked to look at things that the people who found them think are fossils but are really just rocks that look a little like fossils.

Karen: It is common to find modern animal bones when you are looking for dinosaur bones. Fortunately, it is pretty easy to tell ancient bones from modern bones because ancient bones are usually highly mineralized and heavy. The real challenge is trying to identify a particular type of dinosaur when you only have a small piece of one of its bones.

I want to be a paleontologist when I grow up. What should I do?

Karen: Take as many science classes as you can! Biology and geology courses are particularly important, but some paleontologists use their knowledge of chemistry, engineering, statistics, and other fields to learn about extinct animals and the habitats they lived in.

Justin: Learn to write clearly! If you can't express yourself so that others can understand you, you won't be able to tell other people about what you've found and why it's important.

DINOS IN DETAIL

Did you know that more than 1,500 species of dinosaurs have been named, from all around the world? It can get confusing to keep all these incredible creatures organized, but most dinosaurs can be classified into a few main groups. Here is a handy guide to help you understand the different families and types of dinosaurs.

THEROPODS

EARLY THEROPODS

Time: Late Triassic to Early Jurassic
Places: southern Africa, southern China, western Europe, southwestern United States
Description: long necks; short arms and legs; relatively small heads and teeth; 6 to 24 feet long
Examples: *Coelophysis, Dilophosaurus, Sinosaurus*

CERATOSAURS

Time: Middle Jurassic to Late Cretaceous
Places: northern Africa, Argentina, India, Madagascar, western United States
Description: many had crests, knobs, or horns on their heads; arms almost useless in some (abelisaurs), but large claws in others (noasaurs); short legs; 6 to 30 feet long
Examples: *Abelisaurus, Carnotaurus, Ceratosaurus, Majungasaurus, Noasaurus*

MEGALOSAURS AND SPINOSAURS

Time: Middle Jurassic (megalosaurs) into the Late Cretaceous (spinosaurs)
Places: Europe (megalosaurs); northern Africa, Argentina, southeast Asia, and England (spinosaurs)
Description: large powerful heads for megalosaurs, long skinny heads for spinosaurs; hands with large claws; tall back spines and short hind legs for some spinosaurs, which may have been aquatic; 20 to 50 feet long
Examples: *Baryonyx, Megalosaurus, Spinosaurus, Suchomimus*

CARNOSAURS

Time: Middle Jurassic into the Late Cretaceous
Places: northern Africa, Argentina, China, western United States
Description: similar to megalosaurs but with thicker, more powerful bodies; 20 to 40 feet long
Examples: *Acrocanthosaurus, Allosaurus, Carcharodontosaurus, Giganotosaurus*

TYRANNOSAURS

Time: Middle Jurassic ancestors, but not spreading until Late Cretaceous

Places: China, Mongolia, western North America

Description: similar to carnosaurs but with stronger skulls, shorter arms (many had hands with only two fingers), and longer legs; 20 to 40 feet long

Examples: *Albertosaurus*, *Daspletosaurus*, *Gorgosaurus*, *Tarbosaurus*, *Tyrannosaurus*

ORNITHOMIMOSAURS

Time: Cretaceous

Places: China, Mongolia, western North America

Description: ostrichlike bodies, except with long clawed arms and long bony tails; small heads (almost always toothless) and long flexible necks; mostly 6 to 15 feet long (35-foot-long duckbill-like *Deinocheirus* the exception); probably herbivores to omnivores

Examples: *Deinocheirus*, *Gallimimus*, *Ornithomimus*, *Struthiomimus*

THERIZINOSAURS

Time: Cretaceous

Places: China, Mongolia, western North America

Description: funny looking, with small heads, long necks, long arms, short legs, and short tails; mostly 10 to 20 feet long, up to 35 feet; probably herbivores

Examples: *Segnosaurus*, *Therizinosaurus*

OVIRAPTOROSAURS

Time: Cretaceous

Places: China, Mongolia, western North America

Description: small toothless heads on long necks; often head crests; long arms and legs; short tails; mostly 3 to 9 feet long, but a few much larger (*Gigantoraptor* more than 25 feet long); probably herbivores to omnivores

Examples: *Anzu*, *Avimimus*, *Caudipteryx*, *Chirostenotes*, *Gigantoraptor*, *Oviraptor*

TROODONTIDS

Time: Cretaceous

Places: China, Mongolia, western North America

Description: long heads on long necks; large brains for dinosaurs; long arms and legs; sickle claw on second toe, but not as large as dromaeosaur sickle claws; 3 to 8 feet long; maybe omnivores to carnivores

Examples: *Saurornithoides*, *Stenonychosaurus*, *Troodon*

DROMAEOSAURS

Time: Cretaceous

Places: Argentina, China, Europe, Mongolia, western North America

Description: similar to troodontids, but with larger heads, shorter legs, and larger sickle claws; 5 to 20 feet long

Examples: *Deinonychus*, *Utahraptor*, *Velociraptor*

SAUROPODOMORPHS

PROSAUROPODS

Time: Late Triassic to Early Jurassic

Places: worldwide

Description: small heads; long necks; moderately long arms with large clawed hands; long tails; most walked on two legs, but some moved on all fours; 6 to 30 feet long

Examples: *Anchisaurus*, *Massospondylus*, *Plateosaurus*

SAUROPODS

Time: Late Triassic to Late Cretaceous

Places: Worldwide

Description: Most sauropods are poorly known, and their large bones make them difficult to study, so scientists often disagree on the best ways to divide them. Most sauropods had small heads on long necks, with long tails, and front and hind legs of similar size. Some special groups include: brachiosaurs, with high shoulders and upward necks; diplodocids, with whiplike tails and peg teeth; and titanosaurs, which had broad bodies and sometimes armor. The biggest sauropods were 100 feet or more long and could weigh more than 50 tons.

Examples: *Amargasaurus, Apatosaurus, Brachiosaurus, Brontosaurus, Camarasaurus, Diplodocus, Mamenchisaurus, Saltasaurus*

ORNITHISCHIANS

STEGOSAURS (PLATED DINOSAURS)

Time: Middle Jurassic to Early Cretaceous

Places: China, England, Tanzania, western United States

Description: small heads; moderately long necks; short front legs; high hips; two rows of plates or spikes along the back; 12 to 30 feet long

Examples: *Kentrosaurus, Stegosaurus*

ANKYLOSAURS

Time: Late Jurassic to Late Cretaceous

Places: China, Europe, Mongolia, western North America

Description: small heads, sometimes with short horns at the back; short necks with half-rings of armor; broad flat bodies; various kinds of bony armor, with large spikes on some (nodosaurs) and tail clubs on others (ankylosaurs); 10 to 30 feet long

Examples: *Ankylosaurus, Euoplocephalus, Gastonia, Sauropelta*

ORNITHOPODS

Time: Late Jurassic to Late Cretaceous

Places: worldwide

Description: ranged from small swift two-legged animals to *Shantungosaurus*, a giant duck-billed dinosaur more than 50 feet long; began as two-legged, but duckbills could move on all fours; a few, like *Iguanodon*, had thumb spikes; hadrosaurs (duck-billed dinosaurs) had broad toothless beaks and hundreds of cheek teeth, and often solid or hollow crests; 5 to 50 feet long

Examples: *Dryosaurus, Hypsilophodon, Orodromeus, Oryctosaurus, Thescelosaurus* (unspecialized ornithopods); *Camptosaurus, Iguanodon, Ouranosaurus* (intermediate ornithopods); *Corythosaurus, Edmontosaurus, Maiasaura, Parasaurolophus* (hadrosaurs)

PACHYCEPHALOSAURS (BONE HEADS)

Time: Cretaceous

Places: China, Mongolia, western North America

Description: large heads with rough flat surfaces or domes; short arms; short legs; 6 to 20 feet long

Examples: *Pachycephalosaurus, Stegoceras*

CERATOPSIANS (HORNED DINOSAURS)

Time: Cretaceous

Places: China, Mongolia, western North America

Description: This group is famous for its horns and frills, but many ceratopsians were small, two-legged animals with no horns and no frills or small frills; all had a special extra beak bone; 4 to 30 feet long.

Examples: *Chasmosaurus, Pachyrhinosaurus, Protoceratops, Psittacosaurus, Styracosaurus, Triceratops*

INDEX

A

Aardonyx, 97
abelisaurs, 44, 84, 85
Abelisaurus, 137
Acrocanthosaurus, 137
aetosaurs, 1, 5
African violets, xxi, 67
air plants, 5–6, 15, 16, 102
Albertosaurus, 138
algae, 27
alligators, 2, 5
Allosaurus, xv, 3, 33, 34, 35,
    36, 84, 137
aloe, 49
Amargasaurus, 139
American Museum of Natural
    History (New York), 39
ammonites, xii, 29–30, 84
amphibians, xiii, 1, 2. *See also*
    frogs; salamanders
Amphicoelias fragillimus, 35
Anchisaurus, 138

Anhanguera, 43, 44, 46
ankylosaurs (armored dinosaurs),
    139
    Cretaceous, 44, 64
    fossils, 23, 74, 75
    Jurassic, 34
    toy, 76
    Triassic, 2, 3
Ankylosaurus, 63, 64, 76, 139
Anning, Mary, 30
Anzu, 63, 64, 138
Apatosaurus, 33, 34, 36,
    39, 139
aquatic plants, 24–27
Argentinosaurus, xiii
asteroids, 84, 87, 95
Attenborosaurus, 24
Avimimus, 138

B

Barosaurus, 33, 34
Baryonyx, 137
birds, xii, xiii, xiv, 3, 13, 64, 84
Bone Cabin (Wyoming), 33
"Bone Wars," 23, 35
bones, 80, 101–2
    collecting, 98, 99
    finding, 134, 135
    fossilized, 12, 34, 74
    most common, 65
    underwater, 102, 105
Borealopelta, 75, 76–79
Brachiosaurus, 2, 33, 34,
    87–88, 139
Brachylophosaurus, xv, 73,
    76–79. *See also* Leonardo
    (*Brachylophosaurus*
    mummy)
Brazil, xv, 43, 44, 45
Brontosaurus, 35, 39,
    87–88, 139

C

calla lilies, 67

Camarasaurus, 33, 34, 139

Camptosaurus, 33, 34, 139

Capitol Reef National Park, 13

Carcharodontosaurus, 137

cards, homemade, 117

Carnegie, Andrew, 35

carnosaurs, 137

Carnotaurus, 137

Caudipteryx, 138

Cenzoic Era, xi

ceratopsians (horned dinosaurs),
    44, 64, 66, 75,
    84, 139

ceratosaurs, 137

Ceratosaurus, 33, 34, 137

champsosaurs, 53, 63, 64, 73

Champsosaurus, 75

Chasmosaurus, 139

Checkerboard Mesa, 12

Chin, Karen, 55, 133

Chindesaurus, 1

Chirostenotes, 138

clams, 1, 21, 33, 74

Cleveland-Lloyd Dinosaur
    Quarry, 33, 39, 80

coelacanths, 3, 43

Coelophysis, xv, 1, 2, 3, 5, 137

Coelurus, 33

Como Bluff (Wyoming), 33

composting, 54

conifers

    Cretaceous, 63, 73

    Jurassic, 11, 33, 34, 39

    look-alikes, xxi, 5, 58

    Triassic, 1

Cope, Edward Drinker, 23, 35

coprolites (poop). *See under*
    fossils

coral, xii, 24–27, 46–49

Corythosaurus, 57, 139

Cretaceous Period, xii, 44, 64,
    66–69

    ammonites from, 30

    coprolites (fossilized poop)
        from, 54

    extinction in, 74, 84

    marine reptiles of, 23

    plants of, 49, 67, 71, 79

    pterosaurs of, 45

crocodiles, xii, xiv, 1, 85

    relatives of, 3, 11, 12, 33, 34

    toy, 5

    See also phytosaurs

crocodilians, xii, 12, 63, 64, 73, 75

crustaceans, 43

cycads, xxi, 1, 5, 34, 39, 67

D

Dakotaraptor, 63

Daspletosaurus, 53, 54, 138

Deccan Plateau (India), 83

Deinocheirus, 138

Deinonychus, 5, 138

Denver Language School, 133

deserts, 2, 3, 12, 13, 15–16,
    101–2

Dicynodonts. See *Placerias*

Dilophosaurus, 3, 11, 12, 137

Dinosaur National Monument,
    33, 101

dinosaurs

    appearance of, xiii, 2

    carcasses of, 74

    diets of, xiii, 55

    evolution of, xii, 44

    gender of, 133

    groups of, xiii

    sizes of, xiii, 34, 35, 84, 134

    skeletons, 101–2, 120

    timeline, xi

    toys, customizing, 40

Diplodocus, 2, 33, 34, 35,
    134, 139

dragonflies, 8

dromaeosaurids, 53

dromaeosaurs, 63, 138

Dromomeron, 1

Dry Mesa (Colorado), 33

Dryosaurus, 33, 34, 139

duck-billed dinosaurs. *See*
    hadrosaurs (duck-billed
    dinosaurs)

dung beetles, 53, 54, 135

E

Edmontosaurus, 63, 64, 76, 139

Egg Mountain, 53

eggs, xv, 45, 55, 83, 133

    fossilized, 84, 85

    made from ice, 112

Elasmosaurus, 24

England, xv, 21, 22, 30, 135,
    137, 139

equipment and materials

    box planters, 36, 39

    colored sand, 15, 16, 50

equipment and materials
(continued)
containers, xviii, xxii, xxiv, 27
for customizing toys, 40
dinosaur rubber stamps, 123
driftwood, 24–27
funnels, 50
modeling clay, homemade,
105
papier-mâché, 93
petrified wood, xv, 3
salt dough, 19, 29, 61
succulent potting mix, 49
Wardian case, 66, 69
Eubrontes tracks, 11, 13
Euoplocephalus, 139
extinction, xi–xii, xiii, 2, 29, 74,
84, 87–88, 95

F

ferns, 109
care of, xxiii
Cretaceous, 63, 64
Jurassic, 33, 34, 39
look-alikes, xxi, 67
Triassic, 1, 2, 5–6
fish, 3, 13
bony, 21, 22, 34, 43, 75
garfish, 73, 75
guitarfish, 73, 75
lungfish, 1, 34
flowering plants, xii, 34, 73, 75
Amborella Trichopoda, 65
appearance of, xii, xiv
Cretaceous, 63, 64, 65,
66–69

grasses as, 85
look-alikes, xxi
trees, 71
forests, 5–6, 57–58, 64, 65,
66–69
formations
Chinle, 1, 2, 3
Hell Creek, 63
Judith River, 73, 75, 79
Kayenta, 12
Lameta, 83, 84, 85
Lance, 63
Lias Group, 21, 22, 30
Moenave/Wingate Sandstone,
11
Morrison, xiv, 33, 34, 35,
36, 101
Navajo Sandstone, 11, 12, 13
Santana, 43, 44
table of common, xv
Two Medicine, 53, 54, 55
fossils, xiv, 34
ammonites, 29–30
burrows, 13
carcasses, 23
Coelophysis, 3
conulariid, 135
coprolites (poop), 12, 54, 55,
57–58, 61, 135
creation of, 74
destruction of, 75
finding, 98–99
homemade, 105
of invertebrates, 22
mummies, 74, 75, 79
in museums, 98, 99
from rocks, 97
underwater, 102, 133–34

See also tracks (trace fossils)
frogs, xii, xiv, 34
Fruita (Colorado), 33
Fruitadens, 34
Fruitafossor, 34

G

Gallimimus, 138
Garden Park (Colorado), 33
Gargoyleosaurus, 33
Gastonia, 139
Ghost Ranch, 1, 3
Giganotosaurus, 137
Gigantoraptor, 138
ginkgoes, xxi, 33, 34, 39
Glen Canyon National Recreation
Area, 11, 13
Gorgosaurus, 138
Grallator tracks, 11, 13
grasses, 34, 49, 61, 83, 85, 112
gratitude tree, 70–71

H

hadrosaurs (duck-billed
dinosaurs), 44, 54, 64, 74,
75, 84, 139
Harris, Gregg "Roosevelt," 66
Histriasaurus, 102
horned dinosaurs. *See*
ceratopsians (horned
dinosaurs)
Horner, Jack, 133
horsetails, xxi, 11, 34, 39, 67

hydrophytes. *See* aquatic
plants
Hypacrosaurus, 57
Hypsilophodon, 139

I

ichthyosaurs, xii, 22, 23, 30
Ichthyosaurus, xv, 21, 24
Iguanodon, 57, 76, 135, 139
India, xii, xiii–xiv, xv, 83, 84–85,
87, 95, 137
invertebrates, 22
Irritator, 43
Isisaurus, 83, 84

J

Jainosaurus, 83
Judiceratops, 73
Jurassic, xii, xiv, 12, 13, 22,
34–35, 36, 44
Jurassic Coast of Dorset, 21

K

Kentrosaurus, 139
Koskinonodon, 1, 2

L

Laevisuchus, 83
Latimer, David, 66
leaves, 70–71, 75

Leonardo (*Brachylophosaurus*
mummy), 75, 79, 134, 135
Leptoceratops, 63, 64
lizards, xii, xiv, 34, 64, 75

M

Maiasaura, xv, 53, 54, 55,
57–58, 139
Makoshika State Park, 63
Malta, 73
Mamenchisaurus, 139
mammals
Cretaceous, 53, 63, 64
fossils, 98
Jurassic, xii, 33, 34
relatives of, xiii
traces of, 11, 12, 13
Majungasaurus, 137
marine reptiles, 21, 22, 23,
24–27
Marsh, Othniel Charles, 35,
39, 64
Massospondylus, 138
Medusaceratops, 73
megalosaurs, 137
Megalosaurus, 135, 137
Mesozoic Era, xi, xii, xiii–xiv, 29,
45, 54, 65
microbial mats, 11, 13, 134
Mirischia, 43
mosasaurs, xii, 84
mosses, xvii, 39, 67
caring for, 5, 6
Java, 27
in layer cake method, xxii–xxiii
look-alikes, xxi, 39, 67

marimo, 24–27
Spanish, 5–6
Mossy (Jan Brett), 69

N

nature, appreciating, xvii
Noasaurus, 137

O

oceans, 22, 23, 24–27, 45, 46
ornithischians, xiii, 139
Ornitholestes, 33
ornithomimosaurs, 138
Ornithomimus, 138
ornithopods, 139
Orodromeus, 53, 54, 55, 139
Oryctosaurus, 139
Othnielosaurus, 33, 34
Ouranosaurus, 139
Oviraptor, 138
oviraptorosaurs, 138

P

pachycephalosaurs, 139
Pachycephalosaurus, 63, 64,
139
Pachyrhinosaurus, 139
paleontology, 87, 95
as career, 133, 134–35, 136
famous paleontologists, 30,
39

paleontology (continued)
    methods of, 12, 55, 65,
        98–99, 101–2
    See also "Bone Wars"
palms, xxi, 109
Pangaea, xii, xiii, xiv, 35, 44
Parasaurolophus, 57, 139
parties, tips for, 127–28
Permian Period, xii
Petrified Forest National Park,
    1, 2
philodendrons, 27
phytosaurs, 1, 2, 5
Placerias, 1, 2
Placerias Quarry, 1
plants, xvii
    care of, xxiii, xxiv, 5, 6, 16, 66
    Cretaceous, 49, 67, 71, 79
    dessert, 102
    Jurassic, 39
    succulents, xviii, xxiii, 46–49
    table of modern look-alikes,
        xxi
    Triassic, 34
    tropical, 67
    woody, 53
    See also air plants; aquatic
        plants; flowering plants
Plateosaurus, 2, 105, 138
plesiosaurs, xii, 22, 23, 30, 84
Plesiosaurus, xv, 21, 24–27
Polacanthus, 76
Powell, Lake, 13
predators, 35, 45, 64, 66
projects, general guidelines for,
    xvii–xviii
prosauropods, 12, 13, 138
Protoceratops, 139

Psittacosaurus, 139
Pteranodon, 45, 46
Pterodactylus, 45, 46
pterosaurs, xiv, xv
    Cretaceous, 63, 64
    defining, 44
    extinction of, xii, 84
    Jurassic, 21, 33, 34
    projects with, 46–49
    types of, 43, 45

Q

Quetzalcoatlus, 45, 46

R

Rahiolisaurus, 83
Rajasaurus, 83
rays, 43, 44
reptiles, xii, xiii. *See also*
    marine reptiles
Rhamphorhynchus, 45
Riggs, Elmer, 39
rivers and lakes, xiv, 64
    desert, 13
    salt dough, 19
    in terrariums, xxiii, 5–6, 36,
        76–79, 80
rocks, 97, 98, 134. *See also*
    formations

S

safety, xvii
salamanders, xii, 34, 75
Saltasaurus, 139
sand dunes, 12, 15–16
sandbox dig, 120
Santanaraptor, 43
Sauropelta, 139
sauropodomorphs, xiii, 138–39
sauropods, xv, 13, 34, 44, 84,
    85, 87–88, 139
Saurornithoides, 138
Scelidosaurus, 23
scorpions, 11, 12
Scutellosaurus, 11
seashore, 44, 45, 46–49
Segisaurus, 11
Segnosaurus, 138
Seitaad, 11
sensitive plant, xxi, 67
shamrock plant, 67
sharks, 1, 21, 22, 43
Sinosaurus, 137
slime, homemade, 80
snails, 54, 74
snakes, xii, xiv, xv, 83, 85
spinosaurs, 44, 45, 137
Spinosaurus, 3, 137
Stegoceras, 139
Stegosaurus, xv, 33, 34, 35,
    36, 139
Stenonychosaurus, 138
stromatolites, 13
Struthiomimus, 138
Styracosaurus, 139
Suchomimus, 137
Supersaurus, 33

T

Tapejara, 43, 44, 45, 46–49
Tarbosaurus, 138
therizinosaurs, 138
Therizinosaurus, 138
theropods, xiii, 3, 12, 13, 34, 75
    in India, 84
    teeth of, 65
    types, 137–38
Thescelosaurus, 63, 64, 139
titanosaurs, xv, 44, 83, 84, 85
Torosaurus, 63, 64
Torvosaurus, 33, 34
tracks (trace fossils), xv
    fossils of, 11, 12, 13
    homemade, 19
Triassic Period, xii, xiii, 2, 3, 5,
    23, 34
Triceratops, xv, 63, 64, 65,
    66–69, 84, 139
Troodon, 54, 55, 138
troodontids, 53, 73, 138
turtles, xii, xiv, 44, 53, 73, 75
    Cretaceous, 63, 64, 83
    Jurassic, 33, 34
Tweet, Justin, 75, 133
tyrannosaurs, 44, 54, 73,
    75, 138
Tyrannosaurus rex, xv, 3, 63, 64,
    84, 138
    size of, xiii, 34, 54
    skeleton, 134
    teeth of, 65
    toy, 66–69

U

Utahraptor, 138

V

Velociraptor, 3, 5, 138
volcanoes, xii, xiii, 75, 84
    ice cream cake, 124–26
    papier-mâché, 87–88, 93

W

Ward, Nathaniel, 69
water, dechlorinating, 24
Wave, The, 11, 12
workspaces, xviii
wrapping paper, homemade, 123

Z

Zion National Park, 11
Zuul, 73, 97

ABOUT THE AUTHOR & CONTRIBUTORS

ABOUT THE AUTHOR

Christine Bayles Kortsch, PhD, is a writer, teacher, photographer, and mom of two creative boys. She has a PhD in Victorian literature from the University of Delaware and had great fun tromping over the moors and through the museums of England studying embroidery and corsets for her book *Dress Culture in Late Victorian Women's Fiction: Literacy, Textiles, and Activism.* Chritstine has published essays in *Taproot* and *5280 Magazine*, and her succulent designs have been featured in the *Denver Post*. Christine teaches literature and writing at the Rocky Mountain College of Art and Design, and succulent design, terrarium craft, and creative writing at the Denver Botanic Gardens. Her Ink & Stem workshops, which combine creative writing with container gardening, have been named one of the "top 38 cool Colorado classes for adults" by *5280 Magazine*. Christine lives in Denver, Colorado, with her husband, Daniel, two sons, an English springer spaniel named Flora, and five rowdy hens. Learn more at cbkortsch.com.

Justin Tweet, MS, grew up in Minnesota reading about dinosaurs. He earned a Bachelor of Arts degree in geology from the University of St. Thomas and a Master of Science degree from the University of Colorado–Boulder, where he got to work on the gut contents of Leonardo the *Brachylophosaurus*. Today he is a paleontological researcher who documents fossils for the National Park Service, covering everything from Precambrian stromatolites to packrat nests built after the Ice Ages. Justin's favorite dinosaur is the small chunky herbivore *Thescelosaurus*.

Karen Chin, PhD, worked as a seasonal National Park Service interpreter before her interest in ancient life was sparked by working for dinosaur paleontologist Jack Horner at the Museum of the Rockies. This work inspired her to earn her doctorate at the University of California at Santa Barbara with paleobotanist Bruce Tiffney. She has found that her research on Mesozoic ecosystems dovetails with her fascination with the natural environments of today. Karen is now an associate professor and curator of paleontology at the University of Colorado–Boulder.